OPERATI ██████████████████

COURTS OF
HEAVEN

New Edition of a Bestselling Classic on Prayer

Destiny Image Books
by Robert Henderson

365 Prayers and Activations for Entering the Courts of Heaven

Unlocking Wealth from the Courts of Heaven

Resetting Economies from the Courts of Heaven
(mini-book)

Breaking the Stronghold of Iniquity
(with Bill Dennington)

Petitioning the Courts of Heaven During Times of Crisis
(mini-book)

Show Us Your Glory

Praying for the Prophetic Destiny of the United States and the Presidency of Donald J. Trump from the Courts of Heaven

Father, Friend, and Judge

Issuing Divine Restraining Orders from Courts of Heaven
(with Dr. Francis Myles)

Redeeming Your Bloodline
(with Hrvoje Sirovina)

The Cloud of Witnesses in the Courts of Heaven

Prayers and Declarations that Open the Courts of Heaven

Receiving Healing from the Courts of Heaven, Curriculum

Accessing the Courts of Heaven

Unlocking Destinies from the Courts of Heaven, Curriculum

OPERATING IN THE

COURTS OF HEAVEN

New Edition of a Bestselling Classic on Prayer

Granting God
the Legal Rights to
Fulfill His Passion and
Answer Our Prayers

ROBERT HENDERSON

DESTINY IMAGE® PUBLISHERS, INC.
P.O. Box 310, Shippensburg, PA 17257-0310
"Promoting Inspired Lives."

This book and all other Destiny Image and Destiny Image Fiction books are available at Christian bookstores and distributors worldwide.

Cover design by Eileen Rockwell

For more information on foreign distributors, call 717-532-3040.

Reach us on the Internet: www.destinyimage.com.

ISBN 13 TP: 978-0-7684-5449-9

ISBN 13 eBook: 978-0-7684-5447-5

ISBN 13 HC: 978-0-7684-5446-8

ISBN 13 LP: 978-0-7684-5448-2

For Worldwide Distribution, Printed in the U.S.A.

4 5 6 7 8 / 25 24 23

Contents

Introduction 7

Chapter 1   The Three Dimensions of Prayer:
            Approaching God as Father 19

Chapter 2   The Three Dimensions of Prayer:
            Approaching God as Friend 39

Chapter 3   The Three Dimensions of Prayer:
            Approaching God as Judge 51

Chapter 4   Learning to Function in the Courts 69

Chapter 5   The Mountain of the Lord 81

Chapter 6   Bride, Angels, and Worshipers 95

Chapter 7   Registered in Heaven 113

Chapter 8   The Ancient of Days. 123

Chapter 9   The Cloud of Witnesses and the Mediator. . . 133

Chapter 10 The Speaking Blood 145

Chapter 11 Battlefield or Courtroom. 153

Chapter 12 Redeeming Your Bloodline:
            Sin, Transgression, Deceit, and Iniquity 165

Chapter 13   Statute of Limitations 183

Chapter 14   Annulling Covenants and Agreements 191

Chapter 15   Jesus Our Advocate 201

Chapter 16   The Holy Spirit:
              Our Legal Aid 211

Chapter 17   The Books of Heaven 219

Chapter 18   Accessing the Courts by Faith 231

Chapter 19   Partnering with God in the Courts of Heaven 243

Chapter 20   Practical Application 251

Chapter 21   Representing Nations Before the Lord 257

              Questions and Answers 261

              About Robert Henderson 265

INTRODUCTION

WHEN I wrote *Operating in the Courts of Heaven: Granting God the Legal Rights to Fulfill His Passion and Answer Our Prayers*, I was astonished at the immediate response I received. I knew these principles had radically touched my life and the life of my family. I found however that people all over the world were looking for answers that other ideas had not brought them. There was something about this teaching that grabbed people and gave them hope. There were people who still practiced the idea of prayer but with little or even no results. However, because they were faithful people, they were praying and doing the best they could. They were tired, weary, and greatly frustrated, but still praying nonetheless. As these people heard the idea that there was a judicial concept to prayer, it seemed to leap in their spirits. When I would begin to teach in different settings, people would tell me, *"This makes perfect sense. I know this is correct; I can feel it in my spirit plus you're proving it from the Word of God."* These people began immediately to apply these principles, with great numbers getting results they hadn't gotten in years. Everything from loved ones coming home who had not been seen or heard from for years, to people actually being raised from the dead as the Courts of Heaven were appealed to. We received testimony of this from Africa and even one occasion in the United States. There has been and continues to be a consistent stream of testimonies of those who have received their breakthrough.

There was another group also who had just simply given up on praying. They had tried it and hadn't seen any results. It was no longer worth the effort for them. This particular spectrum of people also were stirred. They saw hope in this teaching. They began to apply the idea with many getting the results they had given up on previously. I remember one man writing me a letter and thanking me for writing the book. He shared that his son was in jail and this book had gotten into his hands and those of his fellow inmates. They began to apply the principles and appeal to the Courts of Heaven. Many were being released early and finding mercy in the natural court system. They attributed this to the Courts of Heaven having ruled on their behalf and manifesting through the natural realm. These were people who were without hope yet saw the hand of God move on their behalf. They discovered that God as Judge is more merciful than humans are. This is what David discovered and understood. When God gave him the liberty of choosing the judgment in Second Samuel 24:13-14 as a result of his foolish sin of numbering Israel, he chose to fall into God's hand as Judge and not man's.

So Gad came to David and told him; and he said to him, "Shall seven years of famine come to you in your land? Or shall you flee three months before your enemies, while they pursue you? Or shall there be three days' plague in your

*land? Now consider and see what answer I should take back
to Him who sent me."*

*And David said to Gad, "I am in great distress. Please let us
fall into the hand of the Lord, for His mercies are great; but
do not let me fall into the hand of man."*

David knew that he would get mercies from God that man
would never give to him. He chose the judgment of God over the
judgment of men. This is what the prisoners did. They appealed
to the God of all mercies who desires mercy and not sacrifice. The
result was early releases and lighter sentences. The Lord is using
these principles to manifest His kindness and love and restore
hope to the hopeless.

I also discovered that many influential people heard the principles, read the book, and saw breakthrough in their lives and families. It doesn't matter who we are, or the status someone might
hold in a culture or society, we all have needs. Needs can make
us all cry out to God. I was told of one famous Christian leader
whose daughter had been a part of the ministry, then rebelled, left,
and ran away. The leader took the principles of the book, dealt
with the legal rights the devil was claiming, and saw the daughter
return, repentant and broken before the Lord. Restoration was
set in place and a family and ministry were healed as a result. I
personally have had the privilege of praying with many high-pro-
file leaders about situations in their home or ministry. We have
seen breakthroughs and remedies come to these places. In most
of these, they had been crying to God for years. The immediate
answers they received were amazing and caused these leaders to
thank and adore God for His goodness.

I too have continued to apply these concepts. There are now many books that I have written on the subject. I discovered that the Courts of Heaven can be applied in almost any situation. Therefore, there are books dealing with destiny, prayer, declarations, healing, finances, crises, and other areas, with still many more in the works. All these are issues we can bring into the Courts of Heaven and petition the Lord for decisions on our behalf. As I have practiced the principles, I have continued to mature and grow in the execution of them. I have sought to simplify the whole idea. As the idea began to be embraced, others started teaching it. This has been fine, except where unbiblical ideas have been espoused. For instance, someone was convinced that it was possible to go before the Courts of Heaven and get someone out of hell. I had to tell them this was an impossibility. The scripture is clear in Hebrews 9:27.

And as it is appointed for men to die once, but after this the judgment.

The *judgment* here is the eternal judgment. It is the one where we stand before the Lord in the afterlife. If we know Jesus and have a relationship with Him, then we are welcomed into our eternal habitation. If, however, we have rejected Him and been at enmity with Him, we are condemned and suffer the destruction of hell. This is irreversible. Once we pass from this life and into the next, our deeds follow us. We will be judged on the basis of these deeds. My point is that people have adopted the Courts of Heaven idea and taken it places that in my estimation are unbiblical. For instance, there has been another teaching that we can go before

Courts in Hell and do business there. I don't question that there *might* be a court system in hell. I say this only because satan always copies what God created. He wants to be like God! It therefore wouldn't surprise me that there might be a judicial system in satan's empire. However, if there is, we as believers have *no* business seeking to operate there. The Courts of Heaven is the ultimate place where decisions are rendered. A verdict from this place will irrevocably change life in any situation. I personally would not ever seek to do such a thing as to come before a judicial system of hell.

Then there are those who exalt their *seeing/prophetic* gift above the Word of God. They are coming up with all sorts of strange ideas and doctrine based on something they *saw or encountered* in the spirit realm. The problem is there is no biblical foundation for it. If we forsake the Bible as the foundation of our belief system and function, we will pay a heavy price. It will invariably lead us into error and even deceptive spirits operating in us and through us. I believe in the things of the Spirit. I even believe in mystical encounters. This is because on the other side of the coin, I don't want to cut myself off from the moving of the Holy Spirit and His revelations. As one well-revered man of God said after he heard my teaching on the Courts of Heaven, *"Clearly Robert is reading from a different Bible than the rest of us."* This was his way of saying that he had never seen the truths I was speaking of in the Word of God before I taught them. He was confirming for his people that what I was saying was correct because even though he hadn't seen it before, he now saw it in God's Word. All things must line up with the Word of God that He has given us. If they cannot be verified from the written Word of God, they should be outright renounced or at least held in a high degree of suspicion.

> ## All things must line up with the Word of God that He has given us.

In my opinion, some of the teachings on the Courts of Heaven have gotten away from the Bible because people are trying to *carve out* a place for themselves. In other words, they come up with these ideas to try and distinguish themselves in the midst of all the noise. Therefore, the more different and even strange they are, it makes people pay attention. If you don't think this is right, then just consider *Lady Gaga*. In her early years as a pop star she dressed in all sorts of weird attire. She felt that her music and talent weren't enough to set her apart from the rest. These get-ups gave her the edge she needed to succeed. People paid attention. She is indeed talented, but the strangeness gave her that opportunity to prove it. Many of those who are espousing these strange ideas are simply trying to get an edge. They desire to have a voice. Therefore, they take the Courts of Heaven teaching and add all sorts of weirdness to it. The body of Christ must realize that this is only an effort to be heard. The problem is that *Lady Gaga* was simply trying to be a success in something that is for this life. However, when we are messing with eternal truth and the eternal destiny of people, we must be pure. We will give an account before the Lord of what we have done. Did we bring the truth of God's Word or did we pervert it to simply draw a crowd or following? In James 3:1 we are told that teachers will receive a stricter judgment than others. This is because if they teach wrong stuff they are leading others astray.

> *My brethren, let not many of you become teachers, knowing that we shall receive a stricter judgment.*

The stricter judgment will be based on what was being said and its correctness, but also did these teachers live it out themselves. This is a scary thought but very true. If they have revelation but are not applying it to their lives, then they will be judged on this. My prayer is that I will pass the test in that day of judgment.

In the midst of this, I am truly concerned for how biblically illiterate the body of Christ is. As a result of the seeker-sensitive movement that has watered down truth, today we have a church full of converts at best but not disciples. They are susceptible to error and deception because they have no foundation in the Word of God. Teaching on Sunday morning has been replaced with a feel-good snippet. Very few churches have any form of discipleship in place. This draws people. Maybe even a few ask Jesus into their lives. However, they never become disciples. Converts can and will be deceived. Disciples on the other hand have a foundation in their life that will not allow this. I have a saying that I felt the Lord gave me. *Converts make heaven, but disciples make history.* The Lord desires to have a church that looks like and manifests Jesus. Romans 8:29 tells us that the ultimate goal of God is for Jesus to be the first among many.

*For whom He foreknew, He also predestined to be
conformed to the image of His Son, that He might be the
firstborn among many brethren.*

> **Converts make heaven,
> but disciples make history.**

The ambition of the Lord is to have a company of believers
who manifest and are of the same nature, likeness, and image of
Jesus. The Lord will have a tribe, company, and even nation of
people who reflect Him. This requires that we believe and function in the right thing. In regard to the Courts of Heaven, we
must therefore fight against extremism and outright error. We
must know the Bible and allow it to be our guiding light under-
neath the leadership of the Holy Spirit. We must be committed
to *Spirit and Truth*. This is what Jesus declared in John 4:23-24.

*But the hour is coming, and now is, when the true
worshipers will worship the Father in spirit and truth; for the
Father is seeking such to worship Him. God is Spirit, and
those who worship Him must worship in spirit and truth.*

Notice that our revelation of God that allows us to worship is one of *Spirit and Truth*. This means the Holy Spirit and His revelation are essential to us knowing who God is and how He moves. However, *Truth* is also deeply necessary. Without *Truth* we will misread things in the spirit realm. The devil can slip in and cause us to be led astray by pushing ideas that at their core are true, but brought to extremes become error. Only Spirit and Truth can keep us rightly balanced and moving in the things of God. The problem for many is they want Spirit but have no real regard for Truth. Their Truth is their own experience. This will inevitably lead to deception. The Truth must be from the written Word of God being used by the Holy Spirit to bring revelation, insight, and encounters.

In the midst of the craziness surrounding unbiblical activity, I have watched as people are enraptured with supposed prophetic abilities. Many have felt that because they don't have these *gifts* they cannot function in the Courts of Heaven. Quite honestly, this angers me. Not toward people who sincerely want breakthrough, but toward those who would espouse that they are *needed because of their gift* for someone to get their answer. I watch the sheep of God pursue these and it grieves me. The problem is when people run to these supposedly gifted people for help, they are *amazed* at what is being *seen* about them in the spirit world. However, *no breakthrough comes!* If someone is encountering angels and the Cloud of Witnesses and other heavenly things, *something should change!* The problem is, it doesn't! This is because it's quite often not real, or the one who is prophetically *seeing* all this doesn't have the necessary authority to accomplish anything in the spirit world. It is possible for people to have prophetic gifting but not have sufficient authority to do anything in this place. They are therefore watching a movie in the spirit realm, as it were, but have no right to function in it. It is very possible to have a *gift* but not carry an *authority*. These are two separate things in the spirit realm. We will talk of this more in this book.

I do not consider myself a highly prophetic gifted person. I obviously do have abilities to perceive what the Lord is doing. However, there are others whose gifting far exceeds mine. I have discovered something however in my ten-plus years of operating in the Courts of Heaven. I get more breakthrough doing things *by faith* than all the ones *who are seeing angels and the heavenly creatures.* You can too. Those who would make you believe they are necessary to your breakthrough, *are not!* You have what you need at your fingertips. Luke 10:9 unveils that the kingdom of God is near us. The unseen rule of God is close to us.

> *And heal the sick there, and say to them, "The kingdom of God has come near to you."*

The kingdom of God being near us means *it is within our reach.* We must quit thinking "I cannot do it." Yes, you can. Stop believing you can't move into the realm where the Courts of Heaven is. It is accessible to whomever will believe God and move in faith. The Holy Spirit will help us navigate these realms according to Romans 8:26. The Holy Spirit's leadership and inspiration when we pray will empower us.

> *Likewise the Spirit also helps in our weaknesses. For we do not know what we should pray for as we ought, but the*

*Spirit Himself makes intercession for us with groanings which
cannot be uttered.*

To think we cannot do this is to consider the Holy Spirit
inadequate to our need. He is more than sufficient. Let's step
out in faith and learn how to move in these realms. You plus the
Holy Spirit and the Blood of Jesus need nothing else. God will
strengthen you if you will simply believe. I will be endeavoring to
help with this in the coming chapters.

To think we cannot do this is to consider the Holy Spirit inadequate to our need.

One of the main reason for writing this second edition of
Operating in the Courts of Heaven is to clarify the idea and principles connected to God's judicial system. The truth is, I see them
more clearly now than when I wrote the first book. This book will
help many people to understand this realm of the Spirit and how
we can function there. My hope and prayer is that the understanding gleaned here will allow multitudes of others to get the
breakthrough they so desperately long for. God is the Judge of All
according to Hebrews 12:23.

To the general assembly and church of the firstborn who are registered in heaven, to God the Judge of all, to the spirits of just men made perfect.

We have come to this place in the spirit world as New Testament believers. God as Judge is waiting for us to step into His judicial system and petition the Courts. The result will be decisions rendered, prayers answered, and breakthrough resulting. Let's get started!

Chapter 1

THE THREE DIMENSIONS OF PRAYER:
Approaching God as Father

WHEN I first began to teach on the Courts of Heaven, I was so excited about the idea. I knew I was seeing something that was new and cutting edge, even though it's been in the scripture always. As a result of being so excited about it and the breakthrough I was seeing, I thought this must be the way all praying should be done. Others and I were wondering, *"Maybe the Courts of Heaven is **the** key."* I remember mentioning to a high-level apostolic leader who is a friend—who believed and confirmed my teaching—that I was seeing *the Courts of Heaven* in everything in scripture. His response shocked me. He said, *"This is the way error begins."* I knew he was speaking truth. Anything over-emphasized will become error. No one thing is everything, except Jesus. This was when the Lord began to unveil for me that Jesus, in teaching on prayer, actually placed it in three arenas. In the book of Luke He spoke of approaching God as Father, Friend, and Judge. How we see God has everything to do with the way we approach Him in faith. My perception of who He is will empower me in my prayers and requests. Everywhere Jesus walked, people wanted to *see* who He was. Zacchaeus, who was a tax gatherer, wanted to see who Jesus was. There was something he was looking for that he had never been able to satisfy. Luke 19:1-10 shows his encounter with Jesus as He came into Jericho.

> ## My perception of who He is will empower me in my prayers and requests.

Then Jesus entered and passed through Jericho. Now behold, there was a man named Zacchaeus who was a chief tax collector, and he was rich. And he sought to see who Jesus was, but could not because of the crowd, for he was of short stature. So he ran ahead and climbed up into a sycamore tree to see Him, for He was going to pass that way. And when Jesus came to the place, He looked up and saw him, and said to him, "Zacchaeus, make haste and come down, for today I must stay at your house." So he made haste and came down, and received Him joyfully. But when they saw it, they all complained, saying, "He has gone to be a guest with a man who is a sinner."

*Then Zacchaeus stood and said to the Lord, "Look,
Lord, I give half of my goods to the poor; and if I have
taken anything from anyone by false accusation, I restore
fourfold."*

*And Jesus said to him, "Today salvation has come to this
house, because he also is a son of Abraham; for the Son of
Man has come to seek and to save that which was lost."*

This encounter with Jesus brought salvation to Zacchaeus and his house. It bought him to real repentance, which in turn caused him and all his house to be saved. It all began, however, because he desired to see who Jesus was. Clearly he had heard about Jesus, but here he was coming close to where He was. He wanted to really see Him and know who He really was. The problem was he was *short* of stature. Everyone was much taller than he was. They would block his view of really being able to see Jesus. He therefore climbed into a tree to get a better view. The result was not only could he see Jesus, but Jesus *saw* him.

Zacchaeus was a hated man within Jewish culture, though he was a Jew. He was a tax collector. He worked for the Roman government, which was oppressive and cruel quite often to Jewish people. He exploited his own people for the purpose of gain. Yet he wanted to see who Jesus was. Jesus perceived his longing and called him out of the tree. When the Bible says he was of *short stature*, it is describing his physical attributes. However, I also believe it is speaking of the way he saw himself and even the way others saw him. He didn't measure up. There was always a sense of rejection—both of himself and from others. When we have these ideas about ourselves, it hinders us from *seeing* correctly. These perceptions block our correct view. Many cannot see who Jesus is because of rejection that they carry and have as a perpetual sense. When Zacchaeus climbed into the tree, he repositioned himself above all this so he could see. The result was not only did he see Jesus, but Jesus saw him. If we by faith can get *above* all the rejection issues that want to crowd and block our view of Jesus, we will be surprised and shocked that Jesus is actually calling us. We will be amazed at who Jesus is—one who really loves the rejected and cares for the unwanted. What must Zacchaeus have felt when, in the midst of all who hated him, Jesus acknowledged him? Not only did He acknowledge him, He honored him and went to his house. Whoever is hungry for God will be honored. Hebrews 11:15-16 tells us of those who forsook everything out of their desire for God and His purposes.

> *And truly if they had called to mind that country from which they had come out, they would have had opportunity to return. But now they desire a better, that is, a heavenly country. Therefore God is not ashamed to be called their God, for He has prepared a city for them.*

The Lord is not ashamed to identify and be associated with those who long for the better. In the midst of Zacchaeus' past, he desired and longed for spiritual reality. He was looking to see if Jesus was the answer to these deep cravings of his soul. In his amazement he found that He was. He really did *see* who Jesus was that day. The result was a radical conversion with real repentance associated with it. Zacchaeus did what Jesus didn't even ask him to do. This is what happens when we really see who Jesus is. We are compelled from within to bring our lives into alignment with His. May we all really see who Jesus is.

There also were Greeks who came and requested to *see* who Jesus was in John 12:20-24. They had come up to the Jewish feast to worship. Yet they were still hungering and thirsting for something the rituals couldn't satisfy.

> *Now there were certain Greeks among those who came up to worship at the feast. Then they came to Philip, who was from Bethsaida of Galilee, and asked him, saying, "Sir, we wish to see Jesus."*
>
> *Philip came and told Andrew, and in turn Andrew and Philip told Jesus.*
>
> *But Jesus answered them, saying, "The hour has come that the Son of Man should be glorified. Most assuredly, I say to you, unless a grain of wheat falls into the ground and dies, it remains alone; but if it dies, it produces much grain."*

When Jesus heard that the Greeks/Gentiles were crying to see Him, He began to speak of the hour He would be glorified. He knew the only way Greeks were going to come into the covenant with God was for Him to die, be raised, and ascend back to the Father. This is what He was speaking of concerning a grain of wheat falling into the earth but then resurrecting into great, new, multiplied life. From this exalted place, He would send the Holy Spirit back into the hearts of all who believed on Him. This is what He meant when He spoke of being *glorified*. He would take His place as Lord of all and rule from His position in heaven through the person of the Holy Spirit. Whoever would experience this infilling of the Spirit would drink of that which would satisfy forever. Up until this point when the Greeks came asking, Jesus had understood He was sent only to the Jews. By the mandate and protocol of heaven, the Jews had to be visited first with the opportunity to accept Him. In Matthew 15:24 when a woman of Canaan, who was not of the Jewish race, came to Jesus to heal her daughter, He at first refused. He later did grant her request because of her faith and persistence. His reasoning, however, for His refusal is found in the mentioned verse.

> *But He answered and said, "I was not sent except to the lost sheep of the house of Israel."*

Whoever would experience this infilling of the Spirit would drink of that which would satisfy forever.

Jesus understood that His earthly ministry was only to Israel. However, when He died and was crucified by the Jews, it would open the way for the Gentiles to hear the gospel and be saved. The refusal of the Jewish people of their Messiah opened up the salvation of the Gentile world. Paul spoke of this in Romans 11:15 when he explained the result of the Jewish refusal of Jesus as Savior.

For if their being cast away is the reconciling of the world,
what will their acceptance be but life from the dead?

When the Jews denied Jesus as Savior, the result was the gospel going to the Gentiles. If their rejection of Jesus resulted in the world being reconciled to God, what will be the result of their acceptance of Him? God is not finished with the Jewish nation. He will redeem them as well. The result will be unthinkable and powerful as His covenant people through Abraham are brought into the fold and accept Jesus as Messiah and Savior.

When the Greeks came to Philip and wanted to *see* Jesus and who He was, Jesus knew this longing was indicating His hour had come. He would be given for not just the sins of Israel but the sins of the whole world. His death, burial, resurrection, and ascension would suffice for what was necessary that all, regardless of race, could be saved and belong to God. The Father through His Son reconciled Himself back to the world. Second Corinthians 5:18-19 tells us that Jesus' death on the cross caused every enmity with God to be erased. God reconciled Himself back to the whole world through Jesus on the cross.

Now all things are of God, who has reconciled us to Himself
through Jesus Christ, and has given us the ministry of

reconciliation, that is, that God was in Christ reconciling the world to Himself, not imputing their trespasses to them, and has committed to us the word of reconciliation.

Not only did Jesus die for the Jews, His death was sufficient to reconcile God back to the whole world. This means God is not angry with the world any longer. We as believers need to realize this. God's anger was poured out on Jesus on the cross. Jesus took it for us so that we don't have to. However, it is imperative that those God has reconciled to Himself, accept that reconciliation and reconcile themselves back to God. This is what Second Corinthians 5:20 declares.

Now then, we are ambassadors for Christ, as though God were pleading through us: we implore you on Christ's behalf, be reconciled to God.

What God did for us through Jesus on the cross demands a response. We must choose to accept God's extended hand toward us and extend ours back. Should this not be done, should we snub what the graciousness of God is offering, there will be judgment. The Lord went to the greatest lengths imaginable to redeem us. We must respond and accept all that has been provided through Jesus for us.

When the Greeks came desiring to see Jesus, Jesus understood this. There was a longing that was stirring in the hearts of people for a Savior. Jesus knew that He had to fulfill what was necessary to meet the cry and craving that was resident in all men's hearts. We all desire to *see Jesus!*

When I talk of approaching God in the three dimensions of Father, Friend, and Judge, I am talking about *seeing* God in these three ways. We must have a revelation of the Holy Spirit of God in each of these realms. As we perceive Him as Father, Friend, and Judge, it will open up new places of encounter with the Lord. Our thirst and desire for Him can give birth to revelation that causes us to see Him these ways. Let's look at each one.

> Our thirst and desire for Him can give birth to revelation that causes us to see Him these ways.

FATHER

When Jesus' disciples asked Him to teach them to pray in Luke 11:1-2, He responded with insight that would change them forever.

Now it came to pass, as He was praying in a certain place,
when He ceased, that one of His disciples said to Him,
"Lord, teach us to pray, as John also taught his disciples." So
He said to them, "When you pray, say:

Our Father in heaven,
Hallowed be Your name.
Your kingdom come.
Your will be done
On earth as it is in heaven."

These verses of course are very familiar to many. However, it shouldn't be lost on us that Jesus is instructing us to approach God as our Father. After watching Jesus pray, the disciples were moved with a desire to learn how to pray. One of the best ways to learn to pray is by praying with those who know how. Not only can you glean understanding, but you can also *catch* the anointing to pray. If we are to pray effectively, the empowerment of the Holy Spirit is absolutely essential. Romans 8:26 clearly declares to us that we don't have the ability by ourselves to be effective. We must have the unction and strength of the Spirit of God moving in us and through us.

Likewise the Spirit also helps in our weaknesses. For we
do not know what we should pray for as we ought, but the
Spirit Himself makes intercession for us with groanings which
cannot be uttered.

I can learn certain concepts and ideas about praying. However, I must have the Holy Spirit and His anointing to give me empowerment. This is what I can get when I pray with those who have cultivated this place in God ahead of me. This will accelerate my learning curve and grant me efficiency in prayer much quicker.

As the disciples watched Jesus pray, they wanted to be able to do what they witnessed Him doing. As they requested instruction, Jesus began to teach them to first and foremost approach God as *Father*. Approaching God as Father is basic to all praying. Whatever prayer life I may attain, the depth of it will be determined by my revelation of God as my Father. Many want to side-step this place. However, only when we know God as our loving, benevolent, and kind Father, can we began to tap the depths of prayer He desires us to experience. Romans 8:15 shows Paul teaching us about how this revelation of God as Father develops.

> *For you did not receive the spirit of bondage again to fear,*
> *but you received the Spirit of adoption by whom we cry out,*
> *"Abba, Father."*

Paul refers to the Holy Spirit as the Spirit of Adoption. *Adoption* in Paul's culture was a little different from our culture today. Adoption didn't necessarily mean bringing in a child that was not biologically yours and raising them in your home. Adoption spoke of a child coming to a certain age, usually 30, when the father declared them to be a child that he was well pleased in. They were then given full rights and authority from the father. They had the right to operate fully as one who represented the father and his home. This is what happened to Jesus at the River Jordan. Matthew 3:16-17 shows Jesus being *adopted* by the Father as the Holy Spirit descended on Him from heaven.

When He had been baptized, Jesus came up immediately from the water; and behold, the heavens were opened to Him, and He saw the Spirit of God descending like a dove and alighting upon Him. And suddenly a voice came from heaven, saying, "This is My beloved Son, in whom I am well pleased."

The Holy Spirit comes on Jesus as the Spirit of Adoption. Simultaneously the voice of the Father declares that Jesus is His beloved Son. Jesus is *adopted*. He is now commissioned as the representative of the Father and has full rights and authority to operate in this capacity. This is what the Spirit of Adoption grants to us. Remember that the Spirit of Adoption creates within our heart a cry of "Abba, Father." In other words, we have revelation that God is our Father who loves us and accepts us. From this revelation there is a cry or a power to pray that ensues. The understanding we have of God being our Father strengthens our resolve to come before Him in faith and make requests. This is what happened when Caleb gave his daughter Achsah to Othniel as his wife in Joshua 15:16-19.

We have revelation that God is our Father who loves us and accepts us.

And Caleb said, "He who attacks Kirjath Sepher and
takes it, to him I will give Achsah my daughter as wife."
So Othniel the son of Kenaz, the brother of Caleb, took it;
and he gave him Achsah his daughter as wife. Now it was
so, when she came to him, that she persuaded him to ask
her father for a field. So she dismounted from her donkey,
and Caleb said to her, "What do you wish?" She answered,
"Give me a blessing; since you have given me land in the
South, give me also springs of water." So he gave her the
upper springs and the lower springs.

Othniel fights and wins both the battle and the hand of Caleb's daughter Achsah in victory. When Achsah comes to her new husband, she presses him to ask his new father-in-law for a field. However when they come to her father, she not only asks for the field but the springs of water as well. He gives her both the upper and the lower springs. Perhaps Othniel, who was a mighty warrior, was bashful and reluctant to ask for such a thing; Caleb had already given him his daughter. However Achsah knew her father and his generous heart, asked with boldness for much, and got it. She knew her father and his graciousness toward her. When we know the Father's heart, it will embolden us to ask. We will not be bashful or timid. We will come before Him knowing He delights in those who know His goodness and desire to bless. This will create a faith in us toward the Lord that He will not deny. This is what the Spirit of Adoption creates within us.

Notice also that the cry that is created in us is *Abba Father*. *Abba* is a term of endearment. *Father* is a term of authority. The Spirit of Adoption brings awareness of both of these aspects of

God and His Fatherhood. *Abba* basically would mean Daddy in our culture. When someone is called Daddy, Papa, or other terms, it carries a sense of closeness and intimacy. It communicates a deep place of acceptance and love. This is absolutely necessary for us to approach God as Father. Otherwise we are reluctant to come before Him, unsure of His posture toward us. The revelation that He is our Abba is critical. This is what the prodigal son didn't know about his father. In Luke 15:17-19 we see this son preparing his speech as he contemplates returning to his father's house.

> *But when he came to himself, he said, "How many of my father's hired servants have bread enough and to spare, and I perish with hunger! I will arise and go to my father, and will say to him, 'Father, I have sinned against heaven and before you, and I am no longer worthy to be called your son. Make me like one of your hired servants.'"*

The wayward son can only think that perhaps in a moment of mercy his father might just make him a servant. In his wildest dreams he couldn't fathom that the father would reinstate him or restore him to sonship. Yet when he gets to the house, the father sees him coming and runs to meet him. The boy begins his speech only to have the father interrupt him in Luke 15:20-24. The father does the unimaginable and restores him completely to himself and his house.

> *And he arose and came to his father. But when he was still a great way off, his father saw him and had compassion, and ran and fell on his neck and kissed him. And the son said to*

him, "Father, I have sinned against heaven and in your sight, and am no longer worthy to be called your son."

But the father said to his servants, "Bring out the best robe and put it on him, and put a ring on his hand and sandals on his feet. And bring the fatted calf here and kill it, and let us eat and be merry; for this my son was dead and is alive again; he was lost and is found." And they began to be merry.

The son doesn't even get to finish his prepared talk. The father is so excited about the return of the son that he begins to call for robes, rings, sandals, and a party to erupt. His son was home and nothing could make him happier. This is Abba. The Spirit of Adoption unveils this aspect of who God is in His Fatherhood toward us. This is the *first* thing God wants us to know about who He is in His Fatherhood concerning us.

The Lord also is revealed to be Father by the Spirit of Adoption. This is God operating in His authority. Whereas *Abba* is a term of endearment, *Father* speaks of the authority of God. The one does not negate the other. Even though God is our loving, caring, and life-giving Abba, He is also the one who has all authority. In any home there must be authority. This is what gives order to the home. Without authority that is manifest in discipline, there will be chaos. The discipline is to be from a loving perspective, but must be in place for children to grow up and be prepared for their destiny. If all children ever received was the care of Abba without the discipline of Father, then you would potentially end up with irresponsible people. This is what Hebrews 12:6-8 tells us about God as our Father.

"For whom the Lord loves He chastens,
And scourges every son whom He receives."

If you endure chastening, God deals with you as with sons;
for what son is there whom a father does not chasten? But
if you are without chastening, of which all have become
partakers, then you are illegitimate and not sons.

If we never experience the chastening or discipline of the Lord, then we should question whether we actually are His or not. Whoever really belongs to God will be periodically disciplined by Him. This actually indicates that we are His sons and daughters. It is a sign that He loves and cares for us enough to correct us for our own good. This is flowing from the Fatherhood of God and His authority in our life. Not only is God Abba, but He is also Father and will cause us to be changed at times through His discipline. We know that the glory of God is that which changes us. We are told this in Second Corinthians 3:18. We are changed into His image and likeness, which has always been the intent.

> If we never experience the chastening or discipline of the Lord, then we should question whether we actually are His or not.

> *But we all, with unveiled face, beholding as in a mirror the*
> *glory of the Lord, are being transformed into the same image*
> *from glory to glory, just as by the Spirit of the Lord.*

This is what happened to Isaiah as God was cleansing him to function as His prophet. Isaiah 6:1-7 shows Isaiah being purified while standing in the very glory of the Lord.

> *In the year that King Uzziah died, I saw the Lord sitting on*
> *a throne, high and lifted up, and the train of His robe filled*
> *the temple. Above it stood seraphim; each one had six wings:*
> *with two he covered his face, with two he covered his feet,*
> *and with two he flew. And one cried to another and said:*
>
> *"Holy, holy, holy is the Lord of hosts;*
> *The whole earth is full of His glory!"*
>
> *And the posts of the door were shaken by the voice of him*
> *who cried out, and the house was filled with smoke.*
>
> *So I said:*
>
> *"Woe is me, for I am undone!*
> *Because I am a man of unclean lips,*
> *And I dwell in the midst of a people of unclean lips;*
> *For my eyes have seen the King,*
> *The Lord of hosts."*
>
> *Then one of the seraphim flew to me, having in his hand a*
> *live coal which he had taken with the tongs from the altar.*
> *And he touched my mouth with it, and said:*

"Behold, this has touched your lips;
Your iniquity is taken away,
And your sin purged."

As Isaiah encountered God's intense presence and glory, his own sinfulness and lack of holiness was manifested to him. As he acknowledged this, heaven moved to bring cleansing and purifying to him. He was chastened by the Lord in His glory. The sentence "Woe is me, I am undone" actually means, "I am so evil, I should be destroyed." This is chastening. Not that the Lord wanted him to feel this way, but there was a need for his sin to be exceedingly sinful so that he might repent. In the glory of God, things we would otherwise dismiss and justify become magnified and serious. This is good. It is the goodness of God that is chastening us that we might secure our destiny. This is exactly what happened to Isaiah. As Isaiah humbled himself and repented in the glory of the Lord, he was changed. God in His loving mercy and kindness disciplined Isaiah that he might be a partaker of His glory and function as His prophet. The other thing I would mention is that we must approach the Lord with an *open face*. This means that we are hiding nothing and all things are made available for the Lord's inspection. When we realize the goodness of the Lord, we can with great confidence open our lives to Him. We know that any discipline He would bring is for our good and His glory. He is the perfect Father who does all things well. His discipline is perfect. As we endure and embrace the discipline of the Lord as our Father, it produces in us the character and Christ-likeness that is necessary for our future and His purposes. Hebrews 12:10-11 tells us the end result of the chastening and correction of the Lord.

Any discipline He would bring is for our good and His glory.

For they indeed for a few days chastened us as seemed best to them, but He for our profit, that we may be partakers of His holiness. Now no chastening seems to be joyful for the present, but painful; nevertheless, afterward it yields the peaceable fruit of righteousness to those who have been trained by it.

The correction of the Lord is so we can walk in new levels of holiness and have the peaceable fruits of righteousness. I take this to mean that there is a sustained peace that we begin to experience as a result of the righteousness that is worked into our lives. We are told in Proverbs 16:7 that enemies in our lives are subdued and cease to operate against us when we are in full agreement with the Lord.

When a man's ways please the Lord,
He makes even his enemies to be at peace with him.

The Lord causes that which would rise against us to even be subdued when we are walking in a pleasing way before Him. This is the peaceable fruit of righteousness that we are benefiting from. We must allow the correction of the Father to work in us. His heart of love toward us will cause us to come into divine order as we surrender our lives progressively to His ways and order.

Chapter 2

THE THREE DIMENSIONS OF PRAYER:
Approaching God as Friend

A S Jesus continued to teach the disciples on prayer in Luke 11, He shifted gears from approaching God as Father and began to teach them about coming before God as *Friend*. Luke 11:5-8 records this discourse as Jesus taught them and unveiled these secrets.

> *And He said to them, "Which of you shall have a friend, and go to him at midnight and say to him, 'Friend, lend me three loaves; for a friend of mine has come to me on his journey, and I have nothing to set before him'; and he will answer from within and say, 'Do not trouble me; the door is now shut, and my children are with me in bed; I cannot rise and give to you'? I say to you, though he will not rise and give to him because he is his friend, yet because of his persistence he will rise and give him as many as he needs."*

Jesus begins to speak to them about a man with two friends. One has a need on his journey. The other has the means and strength to meet the need. The idea is we would be the friend who is standing in between these two. We don't have the sufficiency to meet the need of the one seeking to progress on his journey. Yet we know a friend of ours who does. Of course, this friend in this story who has sufficiency would be the Lord. We are the ones standing between the two in a place of intercession. We approach God therefore as friend when we are interceding and standing on behalf of another. When we look at those who were friends of God in scripture, we see this is what they did. Abraham in three places is referred to as the friend of God.

> *Are You not our God, who drove out the inhabitants of this land before Your people Israel, and gave it to the descendants of Abraham Your friend forever?* (2 Chronicles 20:7)

As a result of Abraham being the friend of God, God was faithful and kept His covenant with Israel. He drove out the inhabitants of the land that God promised Abraham his descendants would possess. This is all because God considered Abraham His friend. When we are the friend of God, it works on behalf of our descendants after us.

Isaiah 41:8 also lists Abraham as the friend of God. As a result of this, God cares for the nation of Israel.

But you, Israel, are My servant,
Jacob whom I have chosen,
The descendants of Abraham My friend.

God considered Israel His servant and Jacob the one He had chosen, all because Abraham, their father, was His friend. When one is the friend of God, it has a generational effect and, in this case, even determines the destiny and future of a nation.

The other place Abraham is called the friend of God is James 2:21-23. James makes the case that the faith of Abraham that produced works was part of the reason why Abraham was considered by God to be His friend.

Was not Abraham our father justified by works when he
offered Isaac his son on the altar? Do you see that faith was
working together with his works, and by works faith was
made perfect? And the Scripture was fulfilled which says,
"Abraham believed God, and it was accounted to him for
righteousness." And he was called the friend of God.

Abraham fully obeyed God. His faith produced an obedience that blessed the heart of God. This is the kind of faith that allowed God to deem Abraham righteous. Abraham therefore became known as the friend of God. I am citing these occasions because as the friend of God, Abraham was allowed to stand in between Sodom and Gomorrah and God. Exactly what Jesus spoke of in regard to us approaching the Lord as Friend is seen in this occurrence. Genesis 18:21-33 chronicles this amazing account of God allowing Abraham to be involved in the destiny and future of a people.

> *"I will go down now and see whether they have done altogether according to the outcry against it that has come to Me; and if not, I will know."*
>
> *Then the men turned away from there and went toward Sodom, but Abraham still stood before the Lord. And Abraham came near and said, "Would You also destroy the righteous with the wicked? Suppose there were fifty righteous within the city; would You also destroy the place and not spare it for the fifty righteous that were in it? Far be it from You to do such a thing as this, to slay the righteous with the wicked, so that the righteous should be as the wicked; far be it from You! Shall not the Judge of all the earth do right?"*
>
> *So the Lord said, "If I find in Sodom fifty righteous within the city, then I will spare all the place for their sakes."*
>
> *Then Abraham answered and said, "Indeed now, I who am but dust and ashes have taken it upon myself to speak to the Lord: Suppose there were five less than the fifty righteous; would You destroy all of the city for lack of five?"*
>
> *So He said, "If I find there forty-five, I will not destroy it."*
>
> *And he spoke to Him yet again and said, "Suppose there should be forty found there?"*
>
> *So He said, "I will not do it for the sake of forty."*
>
> *Then he said, "Let not the Lord be angry, and I will speak: Suppose thirty should be found there?"*
>
> *So He said, "I will not do it if I find thirty there."*

And he said, "Indeed now, I have taken it upon myself to speak to the Lord: Suppose twenty should be found there?"

So He said, "I will not destroy it for the sake of twenty."

Then he said, "Let not the Lord be angry, and I will speak but once more: Suppose ten should be found there?"

And He said, "I will not destroy it for the sake of ten." So the Lord went His way as soon as He had finished speaking with Abraham; and Abraham returned to his place.

God allowed and needed Abraham to position himself before Him in intercession. Clearly Abraham is standing between God and Sodom and Gomorrah. He is seeking to mediate and broker a deal with God that would spare this wicked place. We must realize that God initiated this whole scenario by unveiling to Abraham that He was going to destroy the cities. He told Abraham a secret. This is one of the characteristics of being a friend of God. Secrets are revealed and told. John 15:15 shows Jesus declaring His disciples the friends of God.

No longer do I call you servants, for a servant does not know what his master is doing; but I have called you friends, for all things that I heard from My Father I have made known to you.

The thing that made them friends was the secrets Jesus told them that He had heard from the Father. God had told Abraham the secret that Sodom and Gomorrah were to be destroyed. As a result of this secret, Abraham appealed to the Lord to reconsider.

God gave audience to Abraham and agreed to what he requested. This is the power of being a friend of God. We know that Sodom and Gomorrah were destroyed because there were not ten righteous. However, this does not negate the fact that God allowed a mortal man functioning as His friend to determine the future of a people he was representing before the Lord. There are three more things I would point out that Abraham did as the friend of God in this place before the Lord. First, he reminded God of who He is. In Genesis 18:23-25 we see Abraham reverently reminding the Lord of who He is.

God gave audience to Abraham and agreed to what he requested. This is the power of being a friend of God.

And Abraham came near and said, "Would You also destroy the righteous with the wicked? Suppose there were fifty righteous within the city; would You also destroy the place and not spare it for the fifty righteous that were in it? Far be it from You to do such a thing as this, to slay the righteous with the wicked, so that the righteous should be as the

wicked; far be it from You! Shall not the Judge of all the earth do right?"

Abraham points out to God that He is the righteous Judge and the integrity of who He is would demand that any righteous would be spared. The motive of Abraham petitioning God on this basis was a concern for God's reputation in the earth. Abraham cared for the people of Sodom and Gomorrah, but he as the friend of God also cared for God's reputation and testimony. When Abraham sought the Lord on this basis, God listened. We must know how to speak the right language to the Lord as His friends. When we do, we get His attention and grasp His ear. Moses as the friend of God used the same approach in Numbers 14:13-16 after God was moved to destroy the whole nation of Israel because of their constant rebellion.

And Moses said to the Lord: "Then the Egyptians will hear it, for by Your might You brought these people up from among them, and they will tell it to the inhabitants of this land. They have heard that You, Lord, are among these people; that You, Lord, are seen face to face and Your cloud stands above them, and You go before them in a pillar of cloud by day and in a pillar of fire by night. Now if You kill these people as one man, then the nations which have heard of Your fame will speak, saying, 'Because the Lord was not able to bring this people to the land which He swore to give them, therefore He killed them in the wilderness.'"

Like Abraham, Moses besought the Lord on the basis of His reputation and the mark it would leave on it if He killed the nation as a whole. The result was God listening to Moses and heeding his counsel. This again is the power of a friend of God. Moses was considered a friend of God according Exodus 33:11.

> *So the Lord spoke to Moses face to face, as a man speaks to his friend. And he would return to the camp, but his servant Joshua the son of Nun, a young man, did not depart from the tabernacle.*

Moses' friendship with God caused a nation to be spared that would have otherwise been destroyed. However, it was secured because one who was the friend of God knew the secret of appealing to God's concern in the matter. When both Abraham and Moses appealed to God on the basis of His reputation in the earth, this grabbed the attention of the Lord. He listened, hearkened, and regarded the prayer of His friends in both situations.

A second thing Abraham did as the friend of God was he *stood* before the Lord. Genesis 18:22 speaks of Abraham *still standing* before the Lord. In other words, Abraham knew the place he was in at that moment before God and didn't want to miss this opportunity.

> *Then the men turned away from there and went toward Sodom, but Abraham still stood before the Lord.*

There are times as the friend of God we are granted moments and times in His presence. We must learn to recognize this and move strategically. If we miss these times, history becomes something different than it could have been. We must be willing to take advantage of these places and times and intercede in secret before the Lord as His friends. This is what Abraham and Moses both did. In that Abraham *still stood* before the Lord, he was aware of the place God had granted him as His friend. He knew this place was strategic in nature. Being the friend of God wasn't something to brag about. It had a functional responsibility attached to it. God needed Abraham to represent issues in the earth before Him. As His friend, God would hear him when others would not be regarded. As the friend of God, a burden was placed upon Abraham to stand between God and what was appointed for destruction. It was Abraham's job as a friend to seek to change and alter this future. So it is ours as the friend of the Lord.

> It was Abraham's job as a friend to seek to change and alter this future. So it is ours as the friend of the Lord.

The third thing Abraham did as the friend of God was he sought for the boundary in the spirit world. Abraham started with fifty and worked his way to ten. This was because he didn't know where the boundary was in regard to what God would allow. This is what we can also do as well. Many times in prayer, I don't know what I should ask for or how far I should go in my request. I normally use the approach Abraham used. He was very reverent and honoring, yet made requests until he knew the limits. Genesis 18:27 show Abraham walking softly before the Lord, seeking to discern what was allowable.

> *Then Abraham answered and said, "Indeed now, I who am but dust and ashes have taken it upon myself to speak to the Lord."*

Notice the humility as Abraham sought to perceive what he should and should not do. He continues again in Genesis 18:30-31.

> *Then he said, "Let not the Lord be angry, and I will speak: Suppose thirty should be found there?"*
>
> *So He said, "I will not do it if I find thirty there."*
>
> *And he said, "Indeed now, I have taken it upon myself to speak to the Lord: Suppose twenty should be found there?"*
>
> *So He said, "I will not destroy it for the sake of twenty."*

Abraham is being very careful as he presses the boundaries seeking to discern them. This is what we do in prayer as we petition the Lord as our Friend. We see through a glass darkly, we are told (see I Corinthians 13:12). In other words, we are seeking to perceive what is going on in the unseen realm that we are functioning in as the friends of God. God knows this and helps us in our endeavor through the person of the Holy Spirit. As we search for the boundaries, we don't want to stop short, but neither do we want to extend past them and grieve the Lord. This is what Abraham is seeking to balance in this place. Genesis 18:32 shows Abraham asking one more time.

> Then he said, "Let not the Lord be angry, and I will speak but once more: Suppose ten should be found there?"
>
> And He said, "I will not destroy it for the sake of ten."

Abraham clearly is convinced that he has reached the limit of what God would allow. As he asks for ten, God agrees. Literally, God and Abraham together have determined what the future of Sodom and Gomorrah could be. Of course we know it was destroyed because there were not ten righteous found. Yet the lesson learned as a friend of God operating before the Lord is an amazing thing. It is God's passion to have us function in this place, and that we might stand and represent others before Him.

Chapter 3

THE THREE DIMENSIONS OF PRAYER:
Approaching God as Judge

JESUS continues His teaching on prayer in Luke 18:1-8. After He points out the need to approach God as Father and Friend, it is as if He left the disciples to *practice* these two realms of prayer. He then picks the subject back up in these verses seven chapters later.

Then He spoke a parable to them, that men always ought to pray and not lose heart, saying: "There was in a certain city a judge who did not fear God nor regard man. Now there was a widow in that city; and she came to him, saying, 'Get justice for me from my adversary.' And he would not for a while; but afterward he said within himself, 'Though I do not fear God nor regard man, yet because this widow troubles me I will avenge her, lest by her continual coming she weary me.'"

Then the Lord said, "Hear what the unjust judge said. And shall God not avenge His own elect who cry out day and

night to Him, though He bears long with them? I tell you that
He will avenge them speedily. Nevertheless, when the Son of
Man comes, will He really find faith on the earth?"

The scripture declares the reason Jesus spoke this parable/
teaching was to encourage the disciples when prayers weren't
being answered. It would appear that if the disciples had been
practicing the two dimensions of prayer Jesus had given them,
there were at least some of their prayers not being answered. Jesus
is said to speak this teaching to encourage them not to lose heart.
This actually means that they should *not turn coward*. Isn't it
interesting that prayer is a statement of bravery? When we pray,
even when it doesn't seem to work, we are acting in a brave and
faith-filled way. There are times in scripture when God's people
are criticized because they didn't act in a brave way and believe
God. Psalm 78:9 reveals that a portion of God's people, though
equipped with what they needed, turned back in the battle rather
than fight.

The children of Ephraim, being armed and carrying bows,
Turned back in the day of battle.

Instead of using what was in their hand, they ran when the
battle was upon them. They surrendered territory to their enemy
rather than standing and fighting. This was considered a very dis-
honorable thing to do because they had what they needed. They
turned coward instead. This is a similar picture of what Jesus is
painting in regard to prayer. We must know that we have at our
disposal all we need to succeed. We need to simply use what has

been placed in our hands. When Jesus began to place prayer in a judicial system, He was placing everything that would be necessary to fight and win in any and all battles into our hands.

> **When Jesus began to place prayer in a judicial system, He was placing everything that would be necessary to fight and win in any and all battles into our hands.**

The key to *brave praying* isn't a ratcheting up of our will and determination. It is recognizing a secret Jesus unveiled in this story that He told. Jesus wasn't acting as a cheerleader, just trying to emotionally stimulate the disciples. He was actually showing them a mystery to getting unanswered prayers answered. Just like approaching God as Father and Friend is essential to effective praying, approaching God in His judicial system as Judge is equally, if not even more essential. Jesus was not telling this story to picture God as an unjust judge who needed to be convinced. He was telling the story to let it be known that if this widow, through persistence, could get a verdict/decision from the unjust judge, how much more can we get a decision from the Judge of all the earth. Jesus was unveiling the third and decisive realm of prayer—approaching God as Judge.

In this story, this widow has an adversary. The word *adversary* in the Greek is *antidikos*. It literally means "one who brings a lawsuit." It is implying our *legal opponent*. The reason the widow's breakthrough wasn't coming was because there was a *legal* case against her. This brings me to one of the most important statements I will make in this book. *The reason for unanswered prayer that is in agreement with the word of God is **something legal is resisting you in the spirit world**!* If we realize this one truth, principle, and secret, we are on our way to our answers and breakthroughs. This mystery has many ramifications connected to it. It opens the door to new understandings and the way we approach prayer, spiritual warfare, and contending for our destiny and future in God. We are going to talk about how we can function in the realm/ dimension of prayer as we approach the Lord as the Judge. We can become proficient at communing with Him as our Father, our Friend, and as the Judge in His judicial setting.

If we are to function in the judicial system of the Courts of Heaven, we should be aware of the Lord as Judge. Just like we need to know Him as Father and Friend, we must have an awareness and revelation of the Lord as Judge. In Daniel 7:9-10 we see an amazing picture of the Courts of Heaven. Daniel as a seer was able to look into the unseen realm and see this Court. The decisions of this Court actually determined life in the earth.

> *I watched till thrones were put in place,*
> *And the Ancient of Days was seated;*
> *His garment was white as snow,*

And the hair of His head was like pure wool.
His throne was a fiery flame,
Its wheels a burning fire;
A fiery stream issued
And came forth from before Him.
A thousand thousands ministered to Him;
Ten thousand times ten thousand stood before Him.
The court was seated,
And the books were opened.

Notice that the One sitting on the Throne is the Ancient of Days. This is the description of God as the Judge who is ruling over heaven's judicial system. *Ancient* means one who is *venerable and worthy of respect because of age, character, and wisdom.* The Lord as Judge is worthy of our worship, adoration, and obedience because He is God. He always has been and always will be. He is eternal. This Judge is impeccable in His character. He is incapable of corruption or being bought. He will render right decisions. There is no partiality with Him. He will render judgments according to His rule of law. Romans 2:9-11 reinforces that God as Judge will render decisions concerning us that are fair and equal.

Tribulation and anguish, on every soul of man who does evil,
of the Jew first and also of the Greek; but glory, honor, and
peace to everyone who works what is good, to the Jew first
and also to the Greek. For there is no partiality with God.

Even if the Lord wanted to, who He is demands that He show no partiality or respect to persons. He must as Judge render decisions that are impartial and just. The Lord also as Judge is filled with wisdom. This means that in the most difficult of cases He is able to render wise and uncontested decisions. This kind of wisdom was seen in Solomon when the women who had babies came before him. One of the babies had died and the other was still alive. Solomon made an astounding decision to discern who the real mother of the baby was. We see this occurrence in First Kings 3:23-28. Both mothers are contending that the remaining alive baby is theirs. In the wisdom of God, Solomon renders a decision.

> And the king said, "The one says, 'This is my son, who lives, and your son is the dead one'; and the other says, 'No! But your son is the dead one, and my son is the living one.'" Then the king said, "Bring me a sword." So they brought a sword before the king. And the king said, "Divide the living child in two, and give half to one, and half to the other."
>
> Then the woman whose son was living spoke to the king, for she yearned with compassion for her son; and she said, "O my lord, give her the living child, and by no means kill him!"
>
> But the other said, "Let him be neither mine nor yours, but divide him."
>
> So the king answered and said, "Give the first woman the living child, and by no means kill him; she is his mother."
>
> And all Israel heard of the judgment which the king had rendered; and they feared the king, for they saw that the wisdom of God was in him to administer justice.

The wisdom with which Solomon made decisions caused the people to honor and revere him. He made these decisions from God's wisdom and insight. This gives us a picture of the wisdom of God in given matters. The Lord as the Ancient of Days sits on this throne of heaven. He rules the judicial system and make decisions that allow the earth realm to come into His order. We can see this even further in Daniel 7:25-27. We see what would be supposed to be the anti-Christ spirit in operation and seeking to rule the earth.

> *He shall speak pompous words against the Most High,*
> *Shall persecute the saints of the Most High,*
> *And shall intend to change times and law.*
> *Then the saints shall be given into his hand*
> *For a time and times and half a time.*
>
> *But the court shall be seated,*
> *And they shall take away his dominion,*
> *To consume and destroy it forever.*
> *Then the kingdom and dominion,*
> *And the greatness of the kingdoms under the whole heaven,*
> *Shall be given to the people, the saints of the Most High.*
> *His kingdom is an everlasting kingdom,*
> *And all dominions shall serve and obey Him.*

As this anti-Christ spirit seeks to expand its rule, the Courts of Heaven is seated. This means it comes to order and is ready to hear evidence and render verdicts. The Court renders a judgment against this spirit that intends to take over the earth. The result is the saints who have been harassed, attacked, and abused by this spirit and those connected with it are freed. One verdict from the Courts of Heaven delivers the saints from defeat and places them in dominion. God gives the nations of the earth into the dominion of the people of God. This is the result of the Courts of Heaven's activity. We are called by God to function in this Court as a part of its process. Isaiah 43:25-26 gives us a glimpse into its operation and our involvement.

> One verdict from the Courts of Heaven delivers the saints from defeat and places them in dominion.

I, even I, am He who blots out your transgressions for My own sake;
And I will not remember your sins.
Put Me in remembrance;
Let us contend together;
State your case, that you may be acquitted.

The Lord is telling His people to make a case before Him by placing Him as Lord into remembrance. We are to bring cases to the Lord and state them. This will give the Lord the legal right He needs as Judge to render decisions on our behalf. The Courts of Heaven is a real, functioning Court. Even though God is God, He needs cases presented before Him to allow verdicts to be rendered. This is why He is declaring that we must put Him in remembrance by stating our case in this Court. We are a part of the process of this heavenly judicial system.

There are several places in scripture where we clearly see God manifested as Judge. Hebrews 12:22-24 shows the activities of the unseen world that we are a part of. This realm is legal in nature.

> But you have come to Mount Zion and to the city of the
> living God, the heavenly Jerusalem, to an innumerable
> company of angels, to the general assembly and church of
> the firstborn who are registered in heaven, to God the Judge
> of all, to the spirits of just men made perfect, to Jesus the
> Mediator of the new covenant, and to the blood of sprinkling
> that speaks better things than that of Abel.

Much of what is mentioned here is legal. This is because it is describing the activity that surrounds and is a part of the Courts of Heaven. The word *church* is the Greek word *ecclesia*. It is a reference to a *judicial, legislative, and governmental people*. This is what the church is. We are called and set by God as ones who have a right to stand in these places in the unseen world. The *spirits of just men* is a reference to the *great cloud of witnesses* spoken of in Hebrews 12:1.

Therefore we also, since we are surrounded by so great a cloud of witnesses, let us lay aside every weight, and the sin which so easily ensnares us, and let us run with endurance the race that is set before us.

The term *witness* is the Geek word *martus*. It means "a judicial witness." The cloud of witnesses give testimony in the heavenly realm as a part of the Courts of Heaven activity. *Jesus the Mediator of the New Covenant* is also legal language. *Mediator* and *New Covenant* both carry strong judicial reference. *The blood that speaks* infers testimony being given. This *blood is speaking better things than that of Abel.* When we look in Genesis 4:9-12, we see God sentencing Cain for his killing of Abel his brother. This is because of the testimony of Abel's blood.

Then the Lord said to Cain, "Where is Abel your brother?"

He said, "I do not know. Am I my brother's keeper?"

And He said, "What have you done? The voice of your brother's blood cries out to Me from the ground. So now you are cursed from the earth, which has opened its mouth to receive your brother's blood from your hand. When you till the ground, it shall no longer yield its strength to you. A fugitive and a vagabond you shall be on the earth."

The voice of Abel's blood required a judgment against Cain. However, the blood of Jesus is speaking better things than that of Abel. Jesus' blood is crying for forgiveness, mercy, redemption, and kindness. On the basis of Jesus' blood, God has the legal right to forgive and redeem us. We must learn to agree and accept the testimony of Jesus' blood on our behalf. In addition to this, we are told that God is the Judge of all. This scripture doesn't reveal Him as King, Lord, or any other of His worthy titles. It reveals Him as Judge. This is because this scripture is granting us insight into what we have *come to*. This means we are a part of the legal dimension of the spirit world and have a right to function there as New Testament believers. However, in this place we are approaching God as Judge of all. We are called and commissioned by God to operate in this place of legal activity for ourselves, our families, our assignments, and our cultures. We are set by God to present cases that allow decisions so that God's passions might be done in the earth.

Genesis 18:25 shows Abraham appealing to God as the *righteous Judge*. He is reminding God of who He is. He is also acknowledging his faith is this part of His character.

> *Far be it from You to do such a thing as this, to slay the righteous with the wicked, so that the righteous should be as the wicked; far be it from You! Shall not the Judge of all the earth do right?*

Again this is *putting God in remembrance*. This is the way we state cases before Him. Abraham reminds God that as Judge, He must do what is right. The Lord would not allow His anger over the wickedness of Sodom and Gomorrah to cause Him to forget the righteous. This is why God delivered Lot from the city before it was destroyed. Genesis 19:21-29 unveils God delivering Lot because He remembered Abraham. Lot was a righteous man. God could not and would not destroy Sodom and Gomorrah until Lot was safe.

> And he said to him, "See, I have favored you concerning this thing also, in that I will not overthrow this city for which you have spoken. Hurry, escape there. For I cannot do anything until you arrive there."
>
> Therefore the name of the city was called Zoar.
>
> The sun had risen upon the earth when Lot entered Zoar. Then the Lord rained brimstone and fire on Sodom and Gomorrah, from the Lord out of the heavens. So He overthrew those cities, all the plain, all the inhabitants of the cities, and what grew on the ground.
>
> But his wife looked back behind him, and she became a pillar of salt.
>
> And Abraham went early in the morning to the place where he had stood before the Lord. Then he looked toward Sodom and Gomorrah, and toward all the land of the plain; and he saw, and behold, the smoke of the land which went up like the smoke of a furnace. And it came to pass, when God destroyed the cities of the plain, that God remembered Abraham, and sent Lot out of the midst of the overthrow, when He overthrew the cities in which Lot had dwelt.

Abraham had made such a case before God as the righteous Judge that Lot was spared as one esteemed to be righteous. Other parts of his family perished. Lot, however, was delivered. Notice the angel literally said that he *could not* do anything until Lot was in a safe place. This was because God remembered Abraham and Lot was spared. Second Peter 2:7 declares that Lot was just even though he was oppressed with the environment he had subjected himself and his family to.

> *And delivered righteous Lot, who was oppressed by the filthy conduct of the wicked.*

This righteousness and Abraham's case before the Lord allowed Lot to be saved. We can do this same thing before the righteous Judge. We can see verdicts rendered for us and for those we would represent before the Lord.

We can see verdicts rendered for us and for those we would represent before the Lord.

Rachel also saw her barrenness broken as she approached God as Judge in Genesis 30:6.

> *Then Rachel said, "God has judged my case; and He has also heard my voice and given me a son." Therefore she called his name Dan.*

Even though this child came through her handmaiden, she knew God was beginning to undo the barrenness that had afflicted and tormented her. She would later have her own children as well. She credited this turn of events to God having made decisions from His judicial place as Judge. Her cry had been heard in heaven and God had ruled in her favor. The name *Dan* actually means *judge*. She named this child to commemorate and reveal the judicial side of who God is.

Jesus actually functioned in the earth aware of God as Judge. First Peter 2:21-23 says that Jesus' power to remain quiet in times of gross mistreatment came from His awareness of God's righteous judgment.

> *For to this you were called, because Christ also suffered for us, leaving us an example, that you should follow His steps:*
>
> *"Who committed no sin,*
> *Nor was deceit found in His mouth";*
>
> *who, when He was reviled, did not revile in return; when He suffered, He did not threaten, but committed Himself to Him who judges righteously.*

Jesus' persuasion was that God would vindicate and justify Him. Therefore He felt no compulsion to vindicate or justify Himself. What a powerful lesson for us to learn. Otherwise we seek to fight the battles we ought to be allowing God to fight for us. The resurrection of Jesus from the dead was the ultimate vindication. Though men had rejected, God had accepted. This has justified Jesus for all ages. One day He will return as the Judge of all. Jesus was very clear about this. God would Judge the world through Him who had been rejected. Acts 17:31 says Jesus will be the Man through whom God judges the earth. The One who was raised from the dead.

> *Because He has appointed a day on which He will judge the world in righteousness by the Man whom He has ordained. He has given assurance of this to all by raising Him from the dead.*

This is the ultimate justice of the Lord. The One who was judged and rejected will be used to judge all others. This is the vindication and justification of God.

We also see a revelation of God as Judge in Revelation 13:10. Those who have suffered and have been persecuted find the power to endure because of the justice of God.

> *He who leads into captivity shall go into captivity; he who kills with the sword must be killed with the sword. Here is the patience and the faith of the saints.*

The reality that there is justice with God gives the saints faith and patience to persevere. All of this comes from the understanding that God is Judge and will render verdicts for and on behalf of His people. Even in the parable of the unjust judge and widow, Jesus declares God will avenge His own elect. Luke 18:7 of that parable enforces this idea.

And shall God not avenge His own elect who cry out day and night to Him, though He bears long with them?

The elect or those who are the chosen of the Lord get the benefit of God's position and place as Judge of all the earth. The Courts of Heaven is not meant to work against the beloved and accepted but to work for us. As we learn to operate in the Courts of Heaven, we will see ever-increasing breakthroughs come to us, our families, and the assignments given to us from the Lord. We are built and meant to stand in the Courts and present cases before Him. May we take our place and not be moved.

The elect or those who are the chosen of the Lord get the benefit of God's position and place as Judge of all the earth.

Lord, as we come before Your Courts that we petition You as the elect of God. We are those chosen in You before the foundations of the earth. Thank You that You, Lord, are our Father, Friend, and Judge. We by faith take our stand in all of these places of prayer. In particular, we approach You as the Judge of all the earth. May we learn and be empowered to stand before You in Your holy place and present cases in these Courts. Thank You that the blood of Jesus gives us access and acceptance in these holy places. In Jesus' Name, amen!

Chapter 4

LEARNING TO FUNCTION IN THE COURTS

ONE of the things that made the Courts of Heaven such a unique revelation was the way it came. It was not the result of years of deep study. It wasn't great time spent in biblical research or investigating. The whole revelation of the Courts of Heaven came through an encounter with the Lord in my own personal prayer time. The other things I've mentioned concerning biblical study and research helped once I became aware of this dimension. However, the understanding itself was because God unveiled it to me Himself. I didn't know it at the time, but the Lord was granting me a concept that has not only begun to touch this generation but will also affect generations to come. This is what happened to Samson in Judges 15:18-20.

Then he became very thirsty; so he cried out to the Lord and said, "You have given this great deliverance by the hand of Your servant; and now shall I die of thirst and fall into the hand of the uncircumcised?" So God split the hollow place that is in Lehi, and water came out, and he drank; and his

*spirit returned, and he revived. Therefore he called its name
En Hakkore, which is in Lehi to this day. And he judged
Israel twenty years in the days of the Philistines.*

After Samson had slain 1,000 Philistines with the jawbone of
a donkey, he cast it away and began to cry out to God in thirst.
Whether it was real or imagined, Samson felt he was about to die
in his present condition. As he called upon the Lord, the Lord
heard and answered. He split the *"hollow place"* and water came
pouring out. Samson drank and was refreshed and revived. Even
though this *"hollow place"* was literally in the ground and filled
with water, it speaks of us. We each have a *"hollow place"* where
the reservoir of God is. If we have been saved and filled with the
Holy Spirit of God, the same Spirit that raised Christ from the
dead lives in us according to Romans 8:11.

*But if the Spirit of Him who raised Jesus from the dead dwells
in you, He who raised Christ from the dead will also give life
to your mortal bodies through His Spirit who dwells in you.*

We are told that the power of the Holy Spirit in us will give
life to our mortal bodies. Not only does this mean that we can be
healed and redeemed from natural sickness, but that the power of
the Spirit will empower us for supernatural purposes. The key is to
see what is in us unlocked and let out. This is what the *hollow place*
being split speaks about. There is a breaking that will occur deep
in us that will release a flow of divine power that will give us drink.
However, this occurrence didn't just give Samson a drink. The
Bible points out two more important elements to what happened

in this moment. First, we are told this spring is there until *this day*. This means that at the writing of this account in the book of Judges, which could have been even centuries later, this well of water that Samson's cry opened was still flowing. This reveals that the moment of pain that Samson was in produced a cry that opened a spring for generations. In other words, God used the cry of Samson from his place of discomfort and even agony to unlock something not only for him but for future generations. His pain was turned into a prayer that contained this level of power! In fact, the name of this place became known as *En Hakorre*. This in Hebrew means *spring of the caller!* The name of the well that was opened lets it be known that the cry of Samson from his pain unlocked that which people were still drinking from generations later.

> **Perhaps the pain you are in is about God creating a cry that will open a spring that generations to come will partake from and be refreshed by.**

Perhaps the pain you are in is about more than you. Maybe the pain is about God creating the level of a cry that can and will open a spring that generations to come will partake from and be refreshed by. The other thing that happened was Samson judged Israel for 20 years. This seems to be connected to the opening of this fountain. What Samson drank from that day empowered him for 20 years of function.

What I have described is actually what happened to me. After teaching on the Courts of Heaven for ten years at this writing, I can tell you that God is and will use this revelation for generations to come. I can also tell you that what opened to me at the encounter I mentioned with God, I have been living from for ten-plus years as of now. I can very personally relate to this story of Samson and his prayer from pain. None of us want pain and sorrow to touch us. Yet it can be from this kind of pain that God will birth a *spring of the caller*. This is my story.

Mary and I had seen God bless us abundantly. We had known His faithfulness and care over us. Then we entered a time of about three years when everything began to fall to pieces. What I mean by this is that we began to be attacked seemingly on every side—finances, relationships, reputations, lies being told, but especially our children. We have six biological children who were all raised in a Christian home. There was no double standard in our home. What we were in public, we were in private. The reason I mention this is because quite often children's rebellion can be traced to witnessing a double standard. They watch their parents be one way when the public is watching and a completely different way behind closed doors. This was not true in our home, then or now. Yet our *grown* children were making decisions that we were dismayed about.

One of the things that was greatly distressing was that our son Adam, who had been a successful youth pastor with his wife, had gone through a divorce. The result of this was that he had been cut off from his two-year-old little girl. This was not because of legal issues but because his now ex-wife would not allow him to see her. The natural court system had granted Adam full rights. However, in anger and bitterness the mother was determined to hurt Adam as much as she possibly could. This resulted in a deep depression coming over Adam. I watched Adam lose every sense of divine destiny. He went from being one who wanted to serve God, to one who felt completely worthless and disqualified from serving the Lord. I have to say here that on the day Adam was born, the Lord spoke clearly to me. Adam had been born in the early morning hours. Later in the afternoon, as I was sitting in a chair trying to rest, because we had been up all night, suddenly the word of the Lord came to me. I heard Him say, "How beautiful are the feet of those who bring good news." Of course this is from Romans 10:15.

> And how shall they preach unless they are sent? As it is written:
>
> "How beautiful are the feet of those who preach the gospel of peace, to bring glad tidings of good things!"

At that moment, I knew that this newborn baby was destined and called of God to preach the *good news* of the gospel. We then took him to the church service the following Sunday to have him dedicated. As our apostolic pastor lifted him up, he began to proclaim, *"How beautiful are the feet of those who bring good news."* I had said nothing to anyone about what I had heard. I asked our apostolic pastor after the service *why* he had prayed and said this. His response was, *"Because this is what God says about him."*

I had watched this word play out for two decades with Adam. I had watched as God had taken possession of his heart. I had watched him marry, have children, and become a success in ministry. Now, however, everything had been stripped away and Adam was in a completely ruined and disillusioned place. My response throughout this whole scenario had been to pray. At this time I only knew how to *war* in the spirit world. My whole perspective was that the spirit realm was a battlefield. Therefore, I had bound and loosed. I had opened and shut. I had denied and forbidden and allowed and permitted. However, over a two-year period nothing had changed. In fact, it had only gotten worse. Adam was in a deep place of depression with no heart for the ministry he had been made for. Every day, I would go to prayer in the morning and part of my time would be to war for Adam. I figured I must not have done enough because things weren't changing. I discovered later that this wasn't true. This is a lie that quite often the enemy torments us with. The truth was, I had been faithful to pray and seek God's face for Adam. The issue *wasn't* that I hadn't done enough. The issue was I hadn't done the *right thing*.

Then all of a sudden this one morning, I went to prayer as was my practice. This time as I began to pray for Adam from a battle-field mentality one more time, I heard the Lord say, *"Bring Adam to my Courts."* The truth was, I had begun to see the concept of the Courts of Heaven. However, I didn't realize its power, nor had I tried to operate in the idea. Therefore, when the Lord said this to me, I was uncertain of how or what to do. I knew, however, that if this was the real voice of God, He would lead me and help me. I therefore took a step of faith and began. I had seen that repentance was a necessary thing before the Courts of Heaven. The devil uses sin legally against us. I knew that whatever claim he had against Adam to hold him in this depression had to be legally removed. As a result, I repented on *behalf* of Adam. The truth is, I didn't even know if this was *right* or not. I discovered later that in First John 5:16 we are told that we can pray for those with sin in their life.

> *If anyone sees his brother sinning a sin which does not lead to death, he will ask, and He will give him life for those who commit sin not leading to death. There is sin leading to death. I do not say that he should pray about that.*

This is clear that God will allow us to deal with sin in the spirit world on behalf of another, if it is not a sin unto death. Adam's sin was not a death sentence. Therefore I could come before the Lord and represent Adam before His Courts. I didn't know all of this at the time. I was just moving by faith. I began by repenting on Adam's behalf for his sin. My repentance didn't remove the *need* for Adam to repent. However, it did at least revoke the legal right of the devil to use his sin against him. My repentance on his behalf was sufficient and granted God the legal ability to revoke satan's claims. I began by praying a prayer like this.

Lord, I bring Adam before Your Courts. As I stand here, I repent on his behalf for his failure as a father and husband. I ask for Your blood to speak for Him. I also repent for any lie he has believed about himself. I ask that these lies would be undone. I ask before Your Courts that every untruth he is believing, he would be forgiven for, in Jesus' Name.

As I finished this short yet powerful prayer of about five minutes, I felt a significant shift in the spirit or unseen world. This was something that I had not felt in this period of over two years. I thought that I was done. I had repented for Adam's failure. However, the Holy Spirit then said to me, *"Now you repent."* I thought, *What have I done?* The Lord very graciously said to me, *"You must repent for the words you have spoken in your frustration against Adam to his mother."* I suddenly *knew* that these words I was guilty of were being used by the devil in the Courts of Heaven. I *knew* that the devil was taking my words and saying before the Courts of Heaven, *"Even his own father says this about him."* Wow! I was convicted and brought to shame. Suddenly I knew I was a part of the problem. I began to repent in absolute sincerity for all the negative things I had said about Adam in my frustration. I had spoken words against him because of choices he had made and decisions he had walked out. The Lord was letting me know that these words were being used in the Courts of Heaven against Adam to hold him in depression and keep him from his destiny. I began to pray:

Lord, I repent for every word I have said against Adam. I ask that I might be forgiven and these words might be annulled. I ask that these words would be dismissed and not allowed as evidence against Adam in Your Courts.

Lord, I love my son. I ask that this might be recorded in the Courts. Let him go free from all the negative things I have spoken against him in Jesus' Name.

This again took about five minutes. I again felt this dynamic shift. I didn't know all that was happening, but I knew *something* was moving. I then with great clarity heard the Lord say, *"Now prophesy Adam's destiny."* I would find later that the Lord was leading me through a process of dealing with an issue in the Courts of Heaven. I discovered that I was undoing a case against Adam; then I was presenting a case on his behalf. Through repentance, I was activating the blood of Jesus to speak on his behalf (see Hebrews 12:24). This was causing any and every case against Adam to be removed. When the Lord told me to *prophesy* Adam's destiny, this was the act of presenting a case for him or on his behalf. We must do both to be effective in the Courts of Heaven. Getting a case dismissed is not enough. We must also present a case as well. Even though I didn't know everything I was doing at the time, God through His graciousness was helping me in my weakness. This is what Romans 8:26 declares.

Getting a case dismissed is not enough.
We must also present a case as well.

*Likewise the Spirit also helps in our weaknesses. For we
do not know what we should pray for as we ought, but the
Spirit Himself makes intercession for us with groanings which
cannot be uttered.*

The Lord empowers us in the midst of our weakness in prayer.
When we don't know what or how we should pray, the Holy Spirit
helps us. This is exactly what the Lord was doing as I interceded
in the Courts of Heaven for my son. As I was instructed, I began
to prophesy Adam's destiny. I began by saying:

Lord, as I stand in Your Courts, I declare that Adam is
ordained by You to carry the good news of the gospel. I
declare that his feet are beautiful and glorious as he runs
with the good news of who You are and Your salvation.
I ask, based on this prophetic word, that You will cause
Adam's destiny and purpose to be restored.

As I was prophesying as I was commanded, I suddenly heard the
Lord say, "Rebuke the spirit of depression now!" I therefore said:

I rebuke you, you spirit of depression. I declare you have
no power against my son. I say your rights are revoked
and you are removed right now in Jesus' Name!

This entire process took maybe 15 minutes. I had never
encountered anything like this. I look back and realize the Lord
had walked me through a Courtroom encounter with Him. I had

undone and seen dismissed the case against Adam. I had presented a case on his behalf; then the Lord had allowed me from the Courts of Heaven to render a judgment against the spirit of depression. I got up from my place of prayer and felt strongly that something had happened. One and a half weeks later, Adam called me. As I answered the phone, he said, "Dad, can I talk to you for a moment?" I said, "Sure." He then said to me, "I don't know what happened, but one and a half weeks ago, all the depression suddenly left me. I want to do God's will and want my destiny and future back." I was amazed. I then knew that the exact time when I had dealt with the demonic rights against Adam in the Courts of Heaven, they had been annulled and dismissed. Adam was now free.

The end of this story is that Adam is now pastoring his own church. He took a group of five and they are almost running 300 now. He is being offered other opportunities in the group he is a part of because of the success he carries. He is very much like Joseph in that they are putting things under his care because of his ability to succeed. This is found in Genesis 39:2-4.

> *The Lord was with Joseph, and he was a successful man;*
> *and he was in the house of his master the Egyptian. And his*
> *master saw that the Lord was with him and that the Lord*
> *made all he did to prosper in his hand. So Joseph found favor*
> *in his sight, and served him. Then he made him overseer of*
> *his house, and all that he had he put under his authority.*

He is very successful and has seen God restore family, children, future, and destiny. His statement is that if you want to see an example of the Courts of Heaven in operation, then look at him. The Lord took that which was devastated and destroyed and has completely restored. I like to make this statement: *"What I was not able to do on the battlefield in a two-year period, I accomplished in the Courts of Heaven in 15 minutes."* This is absolutely true. You can expect the same results as well!

Chapter 5

THE MOUNTAIN
OF THE LORD

AFTER I had been teaching on the *Courts of Heaven* for several years, I became aware that I had inadvertently left the impression that the *Courts of Heaven* was a *method* of praying. People were seeking to use it as a formula to get their prayers answered. As I was teaching in a certain place the Lord said to me, *"The Courts of Heaven is not a method of praying but a dimension of the Spirit."* When I heard this, I knew I had to begin to change the way I was expressing our function and operation in these Courts. I realized for the most part that we had a faulty view of what happens when we encounter God and His presence. We think that He comes to us, when in reality we come to where He is. We enter the place where He Himself functions and operates. According to Hebrews 10:19-20, *we enter* the presence and the holy place of the Spirit.

Therefore, brethren, having boldness to enter the Holiest by the blood of Jesus, by a new and living way which He consecrated for us, through the veil, that is, His flesh.

What Jesus did for us provided us with a new and living way to come before Him and His presence. This shows that it is not Him who comes to us, but rather we step into a spiritual realm and approach Him. This is what Jesus was referring to in John 3:13 when He was seeking to instruct Nicodemus about being born again. We have traditionally wrongly thought that Jesus was seeking to educate Nicodemus about the new birth so he could go to heaven when he died. However, Jesus wanted Nicodemus to know that when he came to life in the spirit realm, it would grant him access into the heavenly dimension *now*.

No one has ascended to heaven but He who came down from heaven, that is, the Son of Man who is in heaven.

Jesus, referring to Himself as the *Son of Man*, which means He was speaking of who He was in His humanity, said He had access into heaven now. When the Bible speaks of *heaven*, so often it is not talking of the place we go when we die. It is speaking of the spiritual sphere we can enter right now. Notice that Jesus is telling Nicodemus that as a human alive in a fleshly body, Jesus ascended into heaven, came down from heaven, and is even in heaven right now. This was Jesus revealing that He was living in two dimensions at one time. He was in the natural realm in His physical being but simultaneously in the spirit world. This is why John 5:19 declares that Jesus did what He saw the Father do. He was unveiling that even while He was alive in a human existence in earth, He was functioning in a heavenly place where God is as His Father.

> When the Bible speaks of *heaven,* so often
> it is not talking of the place we go when we
> die. It is speaking of the spiritual sphere
> we can enter right now.

*Then Jesus answered and said to them, "Most assuredly, I
say to you, the Son can do nothing of Himself, but what He
sees the Father do; for whatever He does, the Son also does
in like manner."*

This was Jesus' secret to the supernatural. He *saw* in the spirit
world and agreed with it from the natural world. The result was
signs, wonders, and miracles that occurred on a regular basis. This
is what we are called to as well. This is why Paul said in Ephesians
2:6 that we are seated in the heavenly places where Jesus is.

*And raised us up together, and made us sit together in the
heavenly places in Christ Jesus.*

This is not meant to be just a theological statement. It is meant
to be a spiritual experience. Whatever our function is as natural,

normal humans, we must recognize we have an exalted place in the spirit world. We have been granted access into a spiritual realm where decisions are made that alter the course of history on the earth. If we can see and imagine this place we are functionally in as New Testament believers, we can change life on the planet. When we were born again, access into these unseen realms was granted to us. We were repositioned in these places. Notice that the Bible actually says there are many different places we can step into in this unseen world. This is what Jesus was referring to in John 14:2-3. We have traditionally and religiously thought Jesus was talking about heaven and Him coming back to take us there. This is *not* what Jesus was unveiling. He was speaking of what would happen when the Holy Spirit came on the Day of Pentecost.

> *In My Father's house are many mansions; if it were not so, I would have told you. I go to prepare a place for you. And if I go and prepare a place for you, I will come again and receive you to Myself; that where I am, there you may be also.*

The *Father's House* is speaking of the spiritual place that God dwells in. For instance, my house is where I live. This is what the Father's House is referring to. Solomon spoke of where God dwelt as he dedicated the temple in First Kings 8:27.

> *But will God indeed dwell on the earth? Behold, heaven and the heaven of heavens cannot contain You. How much less this temple which I have built!*

Solomon recognized that the heaven of heavens, which was a term meaning the unseen spiritual world, couldn't contain God. He was too big even for that. However, where He lives in the unseen places is His House or the Father's House. Notice Jesus says in this *House* or realm are *many mansions*. This is a really bad idea being communicated here. As western believers we think Jesus is somewhere in eternity building us a mansion to live in. This is not what He is referring to. As I have traveled and taught in many places in the earth, I have spoken through many translators. They have used their Bibles that are in their languages. In other languages, this verse is normally *not* translated *mansions*. It is normally translated *places or rooms*. In other words, Jesus was not saying we were going to have a mansion in the world to come. He was saying the Father's House, or the spiritual dimensions that God lives in, has many rooms and places that Jesus' blood has granted us access into.

Jesus continues on and says He is *going to prepare a place for us*. This was Jesus declaring that His work on the cross was to open a way to enter spiritual places that only prophets and priests had access to in the Old Testament. New Testament believers were now going to be able to enter places that only a handful had the privilege before. We are granted entrance into the *Holiest of Holies* now because of what Jesus did on the cross through His body and blood. However, Jesus doesn't stop there. He then declares that *He would come again and receive us to Himself*. This is not Jesus speaking of coming again 2,000 years later. He was speaking of Him coming on the Day of Pentecost and the empowerment that would be received to live in two realms at one time. The Baptism of the Holy Spirit empowers us to function in these unseen places.

Jesus actually had told them in John 14:16-20 that it would be Him who would come in the form of the Holy Spirit.

> *And I will pray the Father, and He will give you another Helper, that He may abide with you forever—the Spirit of truth, whom the world cannot receive, because it neither sees Him nor knows Him; but you know Him, for He dwells with you and will be in you. I will not leave you orphans; I will come to you.*
>
> *A little while longer and the world will see Me no more, but you will see Me. Because I live, you will live also. At that day you will know that I am in My Father, and you in Me, and I in you.*

Jesus declared that *He would come to them* in the form of the Spirit of Truth. He then told them that the world would not see Him but they would. This is because the Holy Spirit would come and abide in them. The Spirit would reveal and uncover who Jesus is in all of His glory and splendor. This is all to say that Jesus came to the disciples through the Holy Spirit to empower them to live in two worlds at the same time. He then makes the statement that the purpose for all this is *that where I am you may be also*. Notice that He didn't say that "I will come to where you are," but rather that *where I am you can be there*. This is Jesus letting them know that through all that He would accomplish and the empowerment of the Holy Spirit, they would be able to live in heavenly realms while alive on the earth. This would allow them to shake off the limits of life lived only on the earth. They would be free to experience glory and impart it to others from the unseen world that He had provided them access into. This is an absolutely essential understanding to function in the *Courts of Heaven*. This is because the *Courts of Heaven* is one of the spiritual places we have been granted access into. It is a realm of prayer that allows us to function in the Courts and make requests and petitions there.

We have in scripture an actual depiction and description of this realm. Hebrews 12:22-24 describes the legal place of the spirit world where God is and we are allowed to *come to*. We have mentioned this previously, but I want to go deeper in this. We can gain invaluable insight in the activity that is a part of this place of the spirit.

> But you have come to Mount Zion and to the city of the living God, the heavenly Jerusalem, to an innumerable company of angels, to the general assembly and church of the firstborn who are registered in heaven, to God the Judge of all, to the spirits of just men made perfect, to Jesus the Mediator of the new covenant, and to the blood of sprinkling that speaks better things than that of Abel.

The writer of the book of Hebrews makes an amazing statement. He declares *we have come* to all this activity that is in the spirit world that is operating on our behalf. We have stated previously that this can all be seen as legal activity in a judicial system. This means this is a part of what is going on in the Courts of Heaven. When it says *we have come* to this, it is implying that we are a part of this activity. When we were born again, we were repositioned to function in this heavenly realm. In other words, we are not trying to get there; we are already there. This is one of the biggest mistakes we make as New Testament believers. We keep trying to get to places we have already come to. This means we do not understand or fully appreciate what Jesus has done for us by His atoning work. We must accept by faith the place we have been granted and begin to function there. This is what Romans 5:2 shows us.

> When we were born again, we were repositioned to function in this heavenly realm. In other words, we are not trying to get there; we are already there.

Through whom also we have access by faith into this grace in which we stand, and rejoice in hope of the glory of God.

Jesus and what He has done provides us *access by faith* into a place of the spirit where we already stand. We *stand* in this place but we have to access it by faith. When we are told we have already *come to* a place, we must realize it requires faith on our part to access it. We're there; however, we must exercise faith and activities associated with faith to function in this place. I'm not trying to get somewhere, but I am seeking to function where I already am. Let me therefore show you the activities in the spirit world associated with the Courts of Heaven. This is necessary, because one of the main things we must do is to *agree* with what is happening in this unseen world. Our agreement causes what is happening in the unseen place to manifest in our seen realm. This is actually what the word *confess* implies. Romans 10:9 is one of several places where this word *confess* is used.

> *That if you confess with your mouth the Lord Jesus and*
> *believe in your heart that God has raised Him from the dead,*
> *you will be saved.*

The word *confess* is the Greek word *homologeo*. It means "to say the same thing." It can, however, be used in a legal setting to mean *agreeing testimony*. When we *confess* or release agreeing testimony from the earth with heaven, things are empowered to manifest. Again, this is what Jesus did when He *saw what the Father was doing* and agreed with it in the earth. Heaven was free to come to earth as a result. We need to understand what is happening in the unseen world of the Courts of Heaven, so we can agree and release corroborating testimony.

The first thing we are told is we have come to Mount Zion. Mount Zion is the place the Courts of Heaven operates from. Mount Zion is not a geographical location; it is a spiritual dimension. It is in fact a governmental spiritual dimension. This means that what we do in this realm doesn't just affect our own lives personally, but can have a cultural effect even in nations. We as New Testament believers has been so positioned by God that our activity in the Courts of Heaven can create cultural shifts and change. We see this first in Ezekiel 28:14-16. In this scripture, we see a description of lucifer while he was in a high-ranking angelic role in heaven. It gives us some insight into where and what his function was.

> *You were the anointed cherub who covers;*
> *I established you;*
> *You were on the holy mountain of God;*
> *You walked back and forth in the midst of fiery stones.*
> *You were perfect in your ways from the day you were created,*
> *Till iniquity was found in you.*
>
> *By the abundance of your trading*
> *You became filled with violence within,*
> *And you sinned;*
> *Therefore I cast you as a profane thing*
> *Out of the mountain of God;*
> *And I destroyed you, O covering cherub,*
> *From the midst of the fiery stones.*

Notice that lucifer was positioned on the holy mountain of God, upon the fiery stones. This is a reference to a governmental place of operation. We know this because Isaiah 2:2-3 tells us that the mountain of the Lord's house will be in the top of all other mountains.

> *Now it shall come to pass in the latter days*
> *That the mountain of the Lord's house*

Shall be established on the top of the mountains,
And shall be exalted above the hills;
And all nations shall flow to it.
Many people shall come and say,
"Come, and let us go up to the mountain of the Lord,
To the house of the God of Jacob;
He will teach us His ways,
And we shall walk in His paths."
For out of Zion shall go forth the law,
And the word of the Lord from Jerusalem.

The word *top* is the Hebrew word *roshe*. It means "a governmental head." The mountain of the Lord's house is so set by God that it determines the atmosphere and climate over all other mountains. Mountains speak of that which is governmental in function. This means that the right environment is created so that right decisions can be made from these places that affect and control culture. We know the *mountain of the Lord's house* is Zion because verse 3 tells us this name. *Out of Zion will go forth the law.* Zion is one of the names of the holy mountain of God. Remember that we have *come to Mount Zion* as New Testament believers. We have been set in this place by God to affect and shift climates and atmospheres in the nations of the earth. We can even see this further in Isaiah 56:7 where we are told that as a House of Prayer we are functioning from this mountain.

Even them I will bring to My holy mountain,
And make them joyful in My house of prayer.
Their burnt offerings and their sacrifices

Will be accepted on My altar;
For My house shall be called a house of prayer for all
nations.

God promised to bring us as a House of Prayer to the very place lucifer was kicked out of for his rebellion. This is why satan hates the praying church so much. We have been granted access into the spiritual place he once functioned in. We have been set by God to operate in Mount Zion from a governmental place. Through our operation in the Courts of Heaven we can not only shift things over our lives and families, but also over the culture of nations! So when we speak of Mount Zion, we are speaking of a governmental position in the spirit world. One more scripture to help substantiate this thought. Psalm 110:1-2 tells us that God will rule over His enemies from Zion.

The Lord said to my Lord,
"Sit at My right hand,
Till I make Your enemies Your footstool."
The Lord shall send the rod of Your strength out of Zion.
Rule in the midst of Your enemies!

Zion is a place of the Lord's executing of judgment against all that would resist His will. Zion in this scripture speaks of the place in the spirit but also the people who occupy that place. The Lord will use us as His people from this governmental place to set His divine order over the earth. What a high call and positioning we have been granted. We will see in the next chapters ideas connected to what is in this dimension of the Spirit called a mountain. From this spiritual dimension we can see cultures shifted from the Courts of Heaven. What we do through the empowerment of the Holy Spirit in the *"mountain of the Lord"* allows the Lord the power and right to bring heaven into earth on a cultural level. The result can be a depiction of earth looking more like heaven than like hell. This is God's passion and it is our honor to be a part of the process that God uses.

Chapter 6

BRIDE, ANGELS,
AND WORSHIPERS

THE next thing we have *come to* and are a part of is the *city of the living God, heavenly Jerusalem.* This is the *bride of Christ* and also the *mother of us all.* Revelation 21:9-10 unveils the Lamb's wife as being this city.

> Then one of the seven angels who had the seven bowls filled
> with the seven last plagues came to me and talked with me,
> saying, "Come, I will show you the bride, the Lamb's wife."
> And he carried me away in the Spirit to a great and high
> mountain, and showed me the great city, the holy Jerusalem,
> descending out of heaven from God.

The angel wanted to show John the Lamb's wife. Perhaps John expected to see a beautiful woman. Yet when it was revealed, it was city coming down from heaven. We know that the Lamb's wife is the church. So the city that is being seen is the corporate people of God. The bride of Christ and the heavenly Jerusalem are synonymous with each other. It speaks of the different functions and operations of the same people. On one hand, the wife of the Lamb is called to great intimacy with the Lord and to rule with Him. On the other hand, we are an operating city that has the power to extend the rule of the Kingdom of God. Matthew 5:14 shows Jesus referring to His disciples as a city.

> *You are the light of the world. A city that is set on a hill cannot be hidden.*

A city on a hill is this heavenly municipality or the *hill of Zion.* We are not to be hidden but to be releasing influence into all the earth! We as the people of God have this function. It is only out of our unbridled intimacy with Jesus that our function as the heavenly city is realized. Jesus actually warned the church at Ephesus about losing her first love. Revelation 2:2-5 shows Jesus cautioning this church about having good things in place but obviously having lost the most important thing—a love relationship with her lover and husband.

> *I know your works, your labor, your patience, and that you cannot bear those who are evil. And you have tested those who say they are apostles and are not, and have found them liars; and you have persevered and have patience, and have labored for My name's sake and have not become weary. Nevertheless I have this against you, that you have left your first love. Remember therefore from where you have fallen; repent and do the first works, or else I will come to you quickly and remove your lampstand from its place—unless you repent.*

It is possible to be doing all the right things but be disconnected with the One who loves us and who we are to love the most. Jesus warned that so serious was this issue that if it wasn't corrected, it would cause this church to forfeit its authority. The lampstand would be removed. Revelation 1:20 tells us that the lampstands are the churches.

> It is possible to be doing all the right things but be disconnected with the One who loves us and who we are to love the most.

The mystery of the seven stars which you saw in My right hand, and the seven golden lampstands: The seven stars are the angels of the seven churches, and the seven lampstands which you saw are the seven churches.

To lose the lampstand would mean you ceased to be a church by heaven's standard. The earth would still call it a church, but heaven wouldn't recognize it. The authority that God intended to be carried by this church would be forfeited and negated. The function to be a *city set on a hill* would be removed because the intimacy that was to be had with the Lord had been lost. It is the intimacy with Jesus that makes us a functioning city set on a hill that cannot be hidden.

We are also told that this heavenly Jerusalem is the mother of us all in Galatians 4:26. As the bride of Christ, this heavenly city from its union with Him conceives and gives birth to the purposes of God.

> *But the Jerusalem above is free, which is the mother of us all.*

The Jerusalem from above that is free is speaking to the fact that we have been delivered from the bondage of the law. We no longer seek to please God by obeying the law but by walking in the freedom and liberty of the Holy Spirit. Romans 8:13-15 gives us insight into how we get free from the bondage and fear of rejection associated with the law.

> *For if you live according to the flesh you will die; but if by the Spirit you put to death the deeds of the body, you will live. For as many as are led by the Spirit of God, these are sons of God. For you did not receive the spirit of bondage again to fear, but you received the Spirit of adoption by whom we cry out, "Abba, Father."*

As we come under the dictates and power of the Holy Spirit, He will strengthen us to deal with the deeds of the body that are against the will of God. We put them to death through the empowerment of the Holy Spirit. We do this, not because of a sense of right and wrong from the law, but by revelation of the Holy Spirit. This is what is being referred to as being led by the Spirit. From a loving relationship with God as our Father, we fulfill His will in a place of safety and confirmation that we are His children. It is the Holy Spirit who fashions His nature in us and causes us to long for what He longs for and hate what He hates. When the church with this revelation and awareness comes into union with the Lord, we produce the right things in the earth. Of course, conception, pregnancy, and finally birthing are all the things that qualify someone to be a mother. As heavenly Jerusalem, we are to be bringing forth the purposes of the Lord in the earth. This will involve travail, which speaks of prayer, intercession, and supplication before the Lord. This means that we as the people of God are to bring forth the intent and desire of the Lord by being His womb in the earth. Travail and intercession are a part of functioning in the Courts of Heaven. I have watched as people have entered deep groanings as we step into the Courts of Heaven. Almost without exception, whatever they have desired has been done. This is because the intercession of the church/city/Lamb's wife is speaking in the Courts of Heaven before His Throne.

I remember one occasion when a young man who was not given to emotion asked to be taken before the Courts of Heaven. He was facing the very real possibility of spending time in jail because of a probation violation. As I helped him come before the Courts of Heaven and repent, it became known that violence was an accusation against him. Suddenly without warning this young man began to travail, cry, and groan in prayer and repentance. I knew that the Lord had *granted* him repentance that would allow something unimaginable to happen when he stood before the natural judge.

I was in the courtroom the day this young man went before the judge. I knew what had happened in the spirit realm and was wondering how it would play out in the natural court setting. As the young man's lawyer began to speak, the judge was looking over the paper. The district attorney had asked that the young man spend ten days in jail and then pay fines and be placed by on probation. This had been agreed upon by the young man and the lawyers. However, as the judge looked over the paperwork and heard the argument being presented, he said, "I don't like this. This is a slap on the wrist for what has been done." It looked like things were not going to go well for this young man. I was wondering what had gone wrong. I was sure it would have gone another way. Suddenly the judge stopped, looked at the young man, and said, "Here's what I'm going to do. No jail time. Your driver's licensed is restored. (It had been revoked.) Finish your original time on probation." Then the judge said, "Go home to your wife, get your education, and if I ever see you in the court again, woe be to you."

The judge actually gave him more mercy than was being asked and set him free. This all happened because the travail of God spoke in the Courts. Heaven was able to render a verdict and decision that allowed this young man freedom and liberty. The mercy of God as Judge was manifested in a natural court. The young man and everyone knew it. Even the young man's lawyer, who had said they did not want this particular judge on the case, was amazed. He had been afraid this judge would not be kind.

This lawyer said he had never seen anything like this happen. This was all a result of the Courts of Heaven and the travail of the mother of us all before the Lord to bring forth His purposes.

The next spiritual activity mentioned in this spirit dimension is *an innumerable company of angels*. There is much angelic activity in the legal realm of the Spirit. Whether we *see* them or not, they are present. We are told that angels have many functions. We know according to Hebrews 1:13-14 they are ministering spirits to minister to those who belong to God.

> But to which of the angels has He ever said:
>
> "Sit at My right hand,
> Till I make Your enemies Your footstool"?
>
> Are they not all ministering spirits sent forth to minister for those who will inherit salvation?

The Lord sends His angels to help us in our weakness. Remember in Luke 22:42-44 when Jesus was in the garden prior to His crucifixion, He was wrestling with what was about to happen. As He came to the place of agreement with the will of God, angels appeared and strengthened Him.

> Saying, "Father, if it is Your will, take this cup away from Me; nevertheless not My will, but Yours, be done." Then an angel appeared to Him from heaven, strengthening Him. And being in agony, He prayed more earnestly. Then His sweat became like great drops of blood falling down to the ground.

Notice that He was able to pray more earnestly. It would appear that the presence of the angel gave Jesus added inspiration and power to pray. What Jesus was about to do on the cross and in the resurrection had to first be birthed in the realm of the spirit. Through His struggle and with the angelic help, the assignment was accomplished. Angels come to help us fulfill the will of the Father. They clearly are also here to do the bidding of the Lord. Psalm 103:20-22 gives us insight into some of the things angels do as well.

> ### Angels come to help us fulfill the will of the Father.

Bless the Lord, you His angels,
Who excel in strength, who do His word,
Heeding the voice of His word.
Bless the Lord, all you His hosts,
You ministers of His, who do His pleasure.
Bless the Lord, all His works,
In all places of His dominion.

Bless the Lord, O my soul!

The terms *angels, hosts, and works* all refer to this angelic activity. The term *angel* means "a messenger." It is the Hebrew word *malak*. The word *host* is the Hebrew word *tsaba*. It means "a mass of entities organized for war—an army." The word *works* is the Hebrew word *maaseh*. It means "an action, a product." Angels are messengers who are sent with information, directions, and commands we are to obey. This happened to Philip in the desert. Acts 8:26-27 reveals Philip going into this desert place because an angel sent him there.

> *Now an angel of the Lord spoke to Philip, saying, "Arise and go toward the south along the road which goes down from Jerusalem to Gaza." This is desert. So he arose and went. And behold, a man of Ethiopia, a eunuch of great authority under Candace the queen of the Ethiopians, who had charge of all her treasury, and had come to Jerusalem to worship.*

Philip ended up leading this man to salvation. This one who had great authority returned to the palace of the Queen of Ethiopia. It is said that through his influence the entire palace and royal court came to know the Lord. This was because an angel came to Philip with a message. Angels are messengers sent to us from the Lord. Angels are also a mass together that form a *host*. They are an army sent to wage war. We see where God sent His angel against the armies of Sennacherib. Second Chronicles 32:19-21 shows the Lord releasing His angel to cut off and destroy the leaders and army attacking Israel.

And they spoke against the God of Jerusalem, as against the gods of the people of the earth—the work of men's hands. Now because of this King Hezekiah and the prophet Isaiah, the son of Amoz, prayed and cried out to heaven. Then the Lord sent an angel who cut down every mighty man of valor, leader, and captain in the camp of the king of Assyria. So he returned shamefaced to his own land. And when he had gone into the temple of his god, some of his own offspring struck him down with the sword there.

Through the prayers of the prophet and the king, God sent an angelic warrior who defeated a king and his seemingly insurmountable army. This is the power of the armies of heaven. Nothing can withstand them or stand against them.

The third word *work,* in regard to angelic activity, speaks of angels as created beings of God. They are His product and creation. They also are sent to do His activities. We are told that the angels, the host, and the work all do the bidding of the Lord. They *do His word.* They *heed His voice.* They *do His pleasure.* They *establish His dominion.* The angelic realm is a very active and involved realm with the purposes of God. They are passionate about doing His will.

Angels also are sent from the Courts of Heaven. This *innumerable* company of angels is the representative of the Courts. This happened in the days of Zechariah when he was contending for the rebuilding of the temple in Jerusalem. The temple's construction had come to a standstill. It had been in this place for as much as 17 years. There were several things that allowed this, but two stand out in Zechariah 5:1-4. We see a flying scroll carrying judgments against thieves and liars.

> *Then I turned and raised my eyes, and saw there a flying scroll.*
>
> *And he said to me, "What do you see?"*
>
> *So I answered, "I see a flying scroll. Its length is twenty cubits and its width ten cubits."*
>
> *Then he said to me, "This is the curse that goes out over the face of the whole earth: 'Every thief shall be expelled,' according to this side of the scroll; and, 'Every perjurer shall be expelled,' according to that side of it."*
>
> *"I will send out the curse," says the Lord of hosts;*
> *"It shall enter the house of the thief*
> *And the house of the one who swears falsely by My name.*
> *It shall remain in the midst of his house*
> *And consume it, with its timber and stones."*

The one who is showing Zechariah these things is an angel. Zechariah 4:1 shows this angel coming and awakening Zechariah to a new place in the spirit world.

> *Now the angel who talked with me came back and wakened me, as a man who is wakened out of his sleep.*

This angel is unveiling many things to the prophet Zechariah. One of them is this whole judgment against what is stopping the restoration of God. We should know that many times people experience a beginning place of restoration. However, it seems to stop. This can be because something in the spirit world is granting a legal right to the devil to resist the complete breakthrough that is desired and needed. Through Zechariah's efforts in the Courts of Heaven, and I am sure others as well, a verdict had been rendered. The scrolls that the angel was showing Zechariah were the verdicts, decisions, and judgments of God against liars and thieves. That which was being used to hold up the restoring process of God was being dealt with. Liars and thieves were holding up the recovery of the Lord. Remember that lies had stopped the building process in the first place. In Ezra 4:12-13, we see people against the restoration of Jerusalem and the rebuilding of the temple perjuring themselves before the King Artaxerxes. They convince the king that if Jerusalem is rebuilt, it will rebel against him.

> *Let it be known to the king that the Jews who came up from you have come to us at Jerusalem, and are building the rebellious and evil city, and are finishing its walls and repairing the foundations. Let it now be known to the king that, if this city is built and the walls completed, they will not pay tax, tribute, or custom, and the king's treasury will be diminished.*

Based on this accusation, the king issued a decree to stop the building of the city. Ezra 4:21-24 shows the response of the king to have the building of the city cease. The lies that were told by those who hated the purposes of God caused the intent and desire of the Lord to be frustrated.

> *Now give the command to make these men cease, that this city may not be built until the command is given by me.*
>
> *Take heed now that you do not fail to do this. Why should damage increase to the hurt of the kings?*
>
> *Now when the copy of King Artaxerxes' letter was read before Rehum, Shimshai the scribe, and their companions, they went up in haste to Jerusalem against the Jews, and by force of arms made them cease. Thus the work of the house of God which is at Jerusalem ceased, and it was discontinued until the second year of the reign of Darius king of Persia.*

This was what God was judging when the verdict of the scrolls shown by the angel was released. However, there was also a judgment against thieves. This was against the people of God who were using the resources meant to build the temple for the building of their own houses. Haggai was also a prophet who prophesied during this time period. In Haggai 1:2-7, we see this prophet confronting the people about living in luxury while the house of God was in ruins.

> *"Thus speaks the Lord of hosts, saying: 'This people says, "The time has not come, the time that the Lord's house should be built."'"*
>
> *Then the word of the Lord came by Haggai the prophet, saying, "Is it time for you yourselves to dwell in your paneled*

houses, and this temple to lie in ruins?" Now therefore, thus
says the Lord of hosts: "Consider your ways!

"You have sown much, and bring in little;
You eat, but do not have enough;
You drink, but you are not filled with drink;
You clothe yourselves, but no one is warm;
And he who earns wages,
Earns wages to put into a bag with holes."

Thus says the Lord of hosts: "Consider your ways!"

By this time the house of God and its construction has been
at a standstill for quite some time. The people have taken the
wood and the material that could have been used to build God's
house and have built their houses instead. The prophet is point-
ing out the result of this is lack, need, and not enough. They
are not flourishing; they are simply surviving. This is because
they have in essence *stolen* and *misappropriated* funds that were
designated for the house of God. They are admonished to *con-*
sider their ways. It would seem that what Zechariah the prophet
was seeing concerning the scroll with judgments on one side
against perjurers and judgment on the other side against thieves
involved these issues. The angel had come to Zechariah to help
bring the judgment of God against that which was stopping His
process. The scroll, however, was a flying scroll. This means that
even though a judgment from the Courts of Heaven had been
issued and rendered, it had not landed in the earth. It would
seem that the angelic unveiling it and the prophetic cooperat-
ing with this realm could land the scroll against that which was
resisting God's restoration.

> **Even though a judgment from the Courts of Heaven had been issued and rendered, it had not landed in the earth.**

We need this today. We need to perceive what the angelic is unveiling. We need the awakening from the angelic to perceive the judgments we have secured from the Courts of Heaven against God's passion being fulfilled. It would appear that once the prophetic perceives what our activity in the Courts has released, decrees and declarations can cause these to be enacted and put in place. This will cause anything and everything that is standing against the desire of God for our inner life or even a nation and culture to be revoked and removed. We learn to prophetically cooperate with the angelic and their operation in and from the Courts of Heaven.

We are also told that we have come to the *general assembly*. This term translated from the Hebrew word *paneguris* means "a mass meeting or a universal companionship." This speaks of the worshipers who are upon the *Sea of Glass* in heaven as revealed in Revelation 15:2-4. We see worshipers upon this place in heaven, where the song of Moses is being sung.

*And I saw something like a sea of glass mingled with fire,
and those who have the victory over the beast, over his image
and over his mark and over the number of his name, standing
on the sea of glass, having harps of God. They sing the song
of Moses, the servant of God, and the song of the Lamb,
saying:*

*"Great and marvelous are Your works,
Lord God Almighty!
Just and true are Your ways,
O King of the saints!
Who shall not fear You, O Lord, and glorify Your name?
For You alone are holy.
For all nations shall come and worship before You,
For Your judgments have been manifested."*

We also see this Sea of Glass in Revelation 4:6 where the four creatures are worshiping the Lord perpetually.

*Before the throne there was a sea of glass, like crystal. And
in the midst of the throne, and around the throne, were four
living creatures full of eyes in front and in back.*

Connected to this are the 24 elders who are also worshiping and crying *worthy is the Lamb* in Revelation 4:9-11. From the Sea of Glass there is constant and ongoing worship.

*Whenever the living creatures give glory and honor and
thanks to Him who sits on the throne, who lives forever and*

ever, the twenty-four elders fall down before Him who sits on the throne and worship Him who lives forever and ever, and cast their crowns before the throne, saying:

"You are worthy, O Lord,
To receive glory and honor and power;
For You created all things,
And by Your will they exist and were created."

As this worship proceeds from the Sea of Glass and the *general assembly*, it resonates through the whole of creation. Revelation 5:11-14 shows the worship beginning and impacting all the creation.

Then I looked, and I heard the voice of many angels around the throne, the living creatures, and the elders; and the number of them was ten thousand times ten thousand, and thousands of thousands, saying with a loud voice:

"Worthy is the Lamb who was slain
To receive power and riches and wisdom,
And strength and honor and glory and blessing!"

And every creature which is in heaven and on the earth and under the earth and such as are in the sea, and all that are in them, I heard saying:

"Blessing and honor and glory and power
Be to Him who sits on the throne,
And to the Lamb, forever and ever!"

Then the four living creatures said, "Amen!" And the twenty-four elders fell down and worshiped Him who lives forever and ever.

Notice that the worship that originated at the Throne with angels, creatures, elders, and the tens of thousands times tens of thousands fills that which is in heaven and earth. Real worship always has its conception in heaven. When we worship in the earth effectively, it is because we are touching the worship of heaven. Worship creates the atmosphere that the Courts of Heaven operates in. This is why the four creatures and all others worship around the Throne. The Throne is the place of Courtroom operation. Decisions are made and judgments are rendered. As we worship in the earth with the worship born from heaven, we are able to step into the dimensions of the Courts. We are actually bringing into earth the atmosphere and operation of the Courts. We also are stepping into this dimension where decisions made determine what happens. May we each and all become worshipers of the King and declare His glory from out of heaven.

Real worship always has its conception in heaven. When we worship in the earth effectively, it is because we are touching the worship of heaven.

Chapter 7

REGISTERED
IN HEAVEN

WE also have come to *the church of the firstborn registered in heaven.* This word *registered* is the Greek word *apographo.* It means to "write off—a copy or list." The church that is recognized in heaven is made up of the ones whose names are written in the Lamb's book of life. The fact that we are registered or recognized in heaven gives us the right to stand as individuals and a corporate people in the Courts of Heaven. Just like in a natural court where not just anyone can bring a case and have it heard, so it is in heaven. We must be a people who are recognized or those who are registered. Jesus told His disciples in Luke 10:19-20, when they were rejoicing that the demons were subject to them, to rejoice instead that their names were written in heaven.

> *Behold, I give you the authority to trample on serpents and*
> *scorpions, and over all the power of the enemy, and nothing*
> *shall by any means hurt you. Nevertheless do not rejoice*
> *in this, that the spirits are subject to you, but rather rejoice*
> *because your names are written in heaven.*

It would seem that their power over demons, serpents, scorpions, and all the power of the enemy was a result of their names being written in heaven. This credibility is what gave them this authority. Heaven recognized them. The fact that we as the church are registered in heaven grants us rights and privileges to stand in the Courts of Heaven and present cases. These cases can be for us individually but also for cultures and nations. Jesus said that His *house or church* was meant to be a house of prayer. When He cleansed the Temple in Matthew 21:12-13, He proclaimed that the intent of God was for it to be this house of prayer.

> *Jesus went into the temple of God and drove out all those who bought and sold in the temple, and overturned the tables of the money changers and the seats of those who sold doves. And He said to them, "It is written, 'My house shall be called a house of prayer,' but you have made it a 'den of thieves.'"*

This is a reference to Isaiah 56:7 we saw earlier, where we are told that God's house will be a place of prayer to represent cultures before Him.

> *Even them I will bring to My holy mountain,*
> *And make them joyful in My house of prayer.*
> *Their burnt offerings and their sacrifices*
> *Will be accepted on My altar;*
> *For My house shall be called a house of prayer for all nations.*

Notice that this *house* is to pray for and represent nations before the Lord. This is what is meant by, *"For my house shall be called a house of prayer for all nations."* In other words, as the church we are to stand in the Courts of Heaven and bring cultures of the earth before the Lord. We are so set as His church that is written, registered, and recognized that we can change the destiny and purpose of nations. This is what God was looking for when He agreed with Abraham to spare Sodom and Gomorrah for ten righteous in Genesis 18:32.

> *Then he said, "Let not the Lord be angry, and I will speak but once more: Suppose ten should be found there?"*
>
> *And He said, "I will not destroy it for the sake of ten."*

Ten was actually within Jewish culture and law the number of the Biet Din. This is Hebrew for *House of Government*. It was made up of three chief justices and seven lesser ones. When these ten made a decision, it became the law of the land. God was agreeing with Abraham that if there were ten who could qualify as judicial people, He would have the legal right to spare an entire population of evil and wicked people. A culture would be shown mercy because there was a house of judicial people who had granted Him this right. It's also interesting to note that in Isaiah 56:7, where God's house is a house of prayer, the word *prayer* comes from the root word *palal*. It means "to judge"! We as a judicial people who are registered and written in heaven are to function judicially before the Lord. We are to represent and present cases on behalf of cultures to allow God the right of His will being done.

The sad fact is that without a House of Prayer or a church of the Firstborn registered in heaven, nations will be judged and even destroyed. This is what happened to Sodom and Gomorrah. There could not be found the ten righteous; therefore it was destroyed and stands today as the epitome of the judgment of God. This occurred not just because of the culture's wickedness but also the absence of a church registered in heaven that could represent it before the Lord. This is what happened on 9/11 when terrorists attacked the United States of America in 2001. I didn't realize this until ten years later in November of 2011. After I had been teaching on the Courts of Heaven for one year, I had a prophetic encounter in a dream. I dreamed that a very well-known apostolic leader's wife sent me his official response to 9/11. I remember seeing it in the dream on the letterhead of his ministry. However, at the bottom of the response was a handwritten note from her. She had written what she had seen that had allowed the awful event to occur. She revealed that she had *seen* that just like there are four living creatures at the Throne of God crying out *Holy, Holy, Holy is the Lord God Almighty*, there were four demonic counter-powers crying out *BOC denied, BOC denied, BOC denied*. This was what had allowed 9/11 and the destruction of it to occur.

I woke up from the dream. I arose and tried to figure out what BOC was. I wondered if it was Hebrew, Greek, or some other language. I could find nothing concerning it. I then Googled BOC. To my amazement, I found it was an acronym. It stood for Body of Christ! I realized the Lord was showing me why 9/11 had been allowed to happen. The demonic had developed a case against the Body of Christ that would not allow our prayers to be effective. They were actually denied the right to speak. This was because in

2001 the church had very little if any unity. We were all a bunch of individuals just chasing our own blessings rather than standing for the purposes of God. This allowed the demonic realm, on a very high level, to bring a case against us. Our prayers were denied from effecting and speaking on behalf of our nation. The result was destruction, loss of life, and historic devastation. 9/11 wasn't the judgment of God in the sense of His anger against America, it was the *absence of the church!* Our absence as a House of Prayer before the Lord gave the demonic a right to cry for destruction that not only changed America but the nations of the world. Could 9/11 have been stopped? Absolutely! However, it would have taken a church registered and listed in heaven that had the right to represent its culture before the Lord.

> **The sad fact is that without a House of Prayer or a church of the Firstborn registered in heaven, nations will be judged and even destroyed.**

This brings me to another very important item to understand concerning the church and the Courts of Heaven. I wondered why Abraham, being so powerful before God that he could see the Lord agree to spare Sodom and Gomorrah for the sake of ten, why he didn't just ask God himself to spare it? After all, being the friend of God gave him a tremendous place of influence and power with God. The answer to this question is simple. Abraham was not *from or a part of* Sodom and Gomorrah. The principle is that a church or ecclesia can only represent the culture it is a part of. Remember that the word *church* is the Greek word *ecclesia*. Of course this is what Jesus said He would build in Matthew 16:18.

> *And I also say to you that you are Peter, and on this rock I will build My church, and the gates of Hades shall not prevail against it.*

Historically, the ecclesia was the governmental/legislative/judicial group that met in the city gates and made decisions concerning issues of that city. They were a small yet powerful group that made these decisions. Their operation actually determined life in that city. This is what Jesus said He would build. The ecclesia within a culture may be small, yet it has great power when recognized in heaven. From the position it has been granted, judicial decisions are made that determine life in that city. Abraham, not being a part of Sodom and Gomorrah, could not legally gain mercy from the Lord on its behalf. Only an ecclesia from there could have done that. As a result of no ecclesia being there, it was destroyed.

We must have churches that are *registered* in heaven—a corporate people made up of those whose names are written down in heaven. These alone have the right to represent the culture they are a part of. I have traveled the world teaching these principles, yet I don't have a right to represent cultures I am not a part of in the Courts of Heaven. My job has been to seek to help strengthen the ecclesia of these cultures with this understanding. When they gain these ideas, they become empowered to stand on behalf of their cultures and see them claimed for the kingdom of God. We must have the church of the Firstborn within cultures, registered in heaven to operate in the Courts of Heaven.

> Any responsibility we have in the church is from a stewardship position. The church has been bought and paid for by the sacrifice of Jesus. It is His.

This brings me to a final thought about this registered church. This church is called the church of the Firstborn. This means that it *belongs* to Jesus and has been purchased by His blood, body, and sacrifice alone. We should never forget this. Any responsibility we have in the church is from a stewardship position. The church has been bought and paid for by the sacrifice of Jesus. It is His. This means He alone has the right to determine its look, operation, and mission. He is the head of the church. Without awareness and commitment to this, we will never be the church that can stand before the Lord and represent nations and culture. May God give us grace to operate as the church bought by His blood and purchased with His immense sacrifice.

Lord, as we come into Your Courts, thank You that You allow me to stand in Mount Zion, the Holy Mountain of God. In this governmental, judicial, and legislative realm, we step into the Courts of Heaven. From this place we believe You for judicial renderings that will allow Your will to be done in the earth.

As we stand in the holy place, we agree with the city of the living God, heavenly Jerusalem, the bride of Christ. We come as Your bride and the mother of all You would do in the earth. As we stand in the place with You, may we operate in the authority this place gives us. Through our worship, conception, and birthing, let Your will be born.

Lord, we are mindful of the innumerable company of angels that are here and we are among. We would agree with the angelic presence and all they would be commissioned to do from Your Courts. Allow their empowerment to come to us as we stand in this place. May they help our insufficiency and we be strengthened to see Your desires fulfilled.

Lord, I agree before Your heavenly judicial system with the general assembly. I seek to worship and agree with heaven itself. May our worship originate in heaven and not in earth. I ask that the atmosphere would be created through our worship that would allow the Courts of Heaven to operate. May we out of the place of heaven stand in the realms of Your Courts as the blood-bought believers giving honor and worship to Your Name. Let even our worship be as testimony before You that would speak as incense in Your Courts.

As we stand before You as the church that is registered and recognized before You, we ask that we might operate on behalf of the culture this ecclesia represents. May the culture shift into divine order as a result of this people who have obtained a place before You. Let the right to show mercy be granted because there is a church/ecclesia that can present the case. In Jesus' Name, amen.

Chapter 8

THE ANCIENT OF DAYS

A S we endeavor to operate in the judicial realm of the spirit world, it is very helpful to recognize the activity there. This helps us to activate our faith and function in this place. We have seen in the previous chapter five differ-ent things that are in operation there. We will see four more in this chapter. The next one definitely allows us to understand that this is a judicial place we are a part of. We are told in Hebrews 12:23 that we have come to God, *the Judge of all*. The Lord is not revealed as Savior, Lord, Deliverer, or any other title we might know Him as. The writer referred to Him as *the Judge*. This is interesting because this means we are stepping into these realms and coming before Him as the Judge of all the earth. Daniel 7:9-10 again shows us what the Courts of Heaven looks like in operation.

> I watched till thrones were put in place,
> And the Ancient of Days was seated;
> His garment was white as snow,
> And the hair of His head was like pure wool.
> His throne was a fiery flame,
> Its wheels a burning fire;

A fiery stream issued
And came forth from before Him.
A thousand thousands ministered to Him;
Ten thousand times ten thousand stood before Him.
The court was seated,
And the books were opened.

Notice that the One who is ruling from His Throne is the *Ancient of Days*. The word *Ancient* in the Hebrew means *venerable*. It is speaking to the fact that He is to be honored, worshiped, and esteemed. He is the One who always has been, is, and always will be. This is the One we are coming and presenting ourselves before. We are told in Revelation 22:13 the high and lofty place of who He is and therefore the honor, respect, and fear that should be shown Him.

I am the Alpha and the Omega, the Beginning and the End,
the First and the Last.

From this place God functions as the Judge of All. When we approach Him, we must come with an awe and reverence and present ourselves as His subjects before His Courts. However, we are also His sons and daughters, His elect. As Jesus taught in Luke 18:6-8, we are these *elect* of God. We have a favored place in His Courts.

Then the Lord said, "Hear what the unjust judge said. And
shall God not avenge His own elect who cry out day and

night to Him, though He bears long with them? I tell you that
He will avenge them speedily. Nevertheless, when the Son of
Man comes, will He really find faith on the earth?"

The word *elect* is the Greek word *eklektos*. It means "to select,
be a favorite, the chosen." As we approach the Courts of Heaven
before the Ancient of Days, the Judge of All, we must realize we
are already favored. I am not trying to gain favor. The blood of
Jesus has already granted me this place as the elect of God. We are
accepted in the beloved according to Ephesians 1:6.

To the praise of the glory of His grace, by which He made us
accepted in the Beloved.

The word *accepted* in the Greek is *charitoo*. It means "to endue
with special honor." If we really understood the way we are
esteemed and valued, we would boldly approach the Courts of
Heaven. From this place we would offer our petition before the
Judge of All who is waiting for us to make our request. We will see
later that the blood is speaking for us and granting us access into
these holy places. We can come and petition the Lord to see His
righteous judgments be rendered for us and concerning us. God
as Judge is waiting for us to take our place and offer evidence and
testimony that allows the judgments of the cross to functionally
undo the works of satan. What we are really doing in the Courts
is bringing into place the finished work of the cross. We are activating, implementing, and executing the verdict of Calvary into
a place of full operation. We are setting ourselves into full agreement with all that Jesus legally accomplished by His atoning work.

> ## What we are really doing in the Courts is bringing into place the finished work of the cross.

The cross was the greatest legal transaction of history. It annihilated satan and his works. It was a verdict rendered. However, a verdict not executed into place has no power. This can be manifest through the example of a young man who went through a divorce. There had been a divorce decree set in place that allowed him to have his daughter on a regular basis. The decree allowed him to have her on alternating holidays. On this particular year, he was to have her on the American holiday of Thanksgiving, which occurs in November of every year. When he arrived at the residence to pick her up, the mother would not relinquish her. She refused to give the two-year-old little girl to her dad. The dad then called the police of the area where this was occurring. When the police came, they informed the dad that they did not take children from one parent and give them to another. He then asked who he could call to make his ex-wife abide by the divorce decree. Their answer stunned and astounded him. They responded, "There is no agency to enforce divorce decrees." In other words, there was no way to make this mother abide by the verdict of the courts.

This is exactly what happens so often in the spiritual world. Jesus has died on the cross and has set everything legally in place for salvation, forgiveness, healing, prosperity, deliverance, family life, and all other benefits of the goodness of God. Yet it is a fact that many of us are living far below the standard of that verdict. People live in perpetual condemnation. They live from trauma to trauma and drama to drama with no visible difference in their life than that of the unbeliever. Believers are sick, diseased, and die prematurely. They live in lack, need, and even poverty. Divorce and family breakup occur as well as children taken captive in rebellion, drug addiction, and all sorts of atrocities. The list could go on. This is all occurring in spite of what Jesus has legally done for us on the cross. This is because there has been no one to execute into place the reality of the verdict based on the virtues of the cross. We as the people of God are those who are the elect and have favor before the Lord to stand in His Courts. We as the corporate people of God are the agency or church that has the right to petition the Courts for all that was legally set in place to become functional. The reason we see the travesties we have mentioned and many others in spite of all that Jesus did and accomplished is because there has been no one to demand in the Courts of Heaven the verdict executed into place. We must know how to come before God as the Judge of All and make our case based on Jesus' work and require the verdict to be honored!

This activity before the Judge will allow the fullness of Jesus' work on our behalf to become reality. We can see this in regard to curses. My definition for *curses* is "a spiritual force sent to sabotage your God-intended destiny." Curses can only operate where there are legal rights discovered. Proverbs 26:2 tells us that they are like birds that have to find a place to put their feet down.

> *Like a flitting sparrow, like a flying swallow,*
> *So a curse without cause shall not alight.*

There has to be a *cause* that allows a curse to operate against us. This means something legal is discovered by the devil that allows this to happen. To stop the curse from destroying us and our future, we must deal with this *cause.* You can yell and scream at the curse, try to stop it through physical manipulation and other means, but it will simply keep denying you the right to succeed. However, if the legal right driving it can be revoked and removed, it will end. Success will come and blessings will erupt. The good news is Galatians 3:13 tells us that Jesus became a curse for us and took any and all curses on Himself on the cross.

> *Christ has redeemed us from the curse of the law, having*
> *become a curse for us (for it is written, "Cursed is everyone*
> *who hangs on a tree").*

This scripture would seem to imply that we are now free from curses and all those associated with the results of not keeping the law. This is absolutely true. From a judicial standpoint a verdict has been rendered. This is the stated verdict of the cross of Jesus. However, in Revelation 22:3 we see that in the millennial reign of Christ there will be *no more curse.*

And there shall be no more curse, but the throne of God and
of the Lamb shall be in it, and His servants shall serve Him.

Why are we seeing that in the *future* kingdom of God there
will *then* be *no more curse?* I thought the curse ended according to
Galatians 3:13 when Jesus died on the cross. It did from a legal,
stated verdict position. However, Revelation 22:3 is the full execution of that verdict into place. In the eternal manifestation of
the Kingdom of God, there will be no more curse because the execution of the verdict rendered based on Jesus' activities is *now* fully
in place! Until that time when this will occur, we must take what
Jesus did into the Courts of Heaven and petition God as Judge of
all to allow the verdict to manifest in the earth and our lives. This
is our *job* as the people of God and as His church. As this happens,
we cease to be a people saying we believe things that we are not
possessing. We begin to live in the reality of all Jesus died for us
to have. We must learn to petition the Courts concerning these
things. Remember according to Second Peter 1:3 everything we
need for life and godliness has *already* been given to us.

As His divine power has given to us all things that pertain to
life and godliness, through the knowledge of Him who called
us by glory and virtue.

We take this reality before the Courts of Heaven so that it
will manifest in our lives. We then escape the travesty of being
a people who say we believe things we never experience. We are
able to move into the manifestation of the cross operating in us
and through us.

> **We take this reality before the Courts of Heaven so that it will manifest in our lives. We then escape the travesty of being a people who say we believe things we never experience.**

We can also see in John 16:7-11 one of the main purposes of the coming of the Holy Spirit.

> *Nevertheless I tell you the truth. It is to your advantage that I go away; for if I do not go away, the Helper will not come to you; but if I depart, I will send Him to you. And when He has come, He will convict the world of sin, and of righteousness, and of judgment: of sin, because they do not believe in Me; of righteousness, because I go to My Father and you see Me no more; of judgment, because the ruler of this world is judged.*

When the Holy Spirit was poured out upon us, He came to convince us of sin, righteousness, and judgment. Notice that the sin is one of unbelief. The Holy Spirit is here to wage war against our human condition of unbelief and bring us to faith. He also is here to manifest to us real, true righteousness. He doesn't want us lawless, but neither does he want us in legalism. He will help us to know what is required of us and give us the empowerment to walk it out. He also is here to convince us of judgment. Notice that this is being done because the ruler of this world, satan, has been judged. Through the power of the Holy Spirit, the revelation of the defeat of the devil is made real to us. We recognize what Jesus really did on the cross to destroy the devil and his works. Through the empowerment of the Holy Spirit, we then can approach the Courts of Heaven and see this verdict completely executed into place.

One of the main functions of the Spirit of God is to empower us to operate in the Courts of Heaven to see the verdict implemented into full operation against the powers of darkness. Remember that the Holy Spirit is the *Helper*. This is the Greek word *parakletos*. This word means "intercessor, advocate, legal aid." The Spirit of the Lord is here to give us legal counsel on how to petition the Courts of Heaven and present the works of Jesus on the cross as the chief evidence for decisions to be rendered into place. We do this before God as Judge of All. He welcomes us into His Courts that we might stand and through the wisdom, counsel, and knowledge of the Holy Spirit we present cases before Him. The work of His Son on our behalf will speak and all that He died for will manifest for us. Hallelujah! The Lord is great and greatly to be praised!

Chapter 9

THE CLOUD OF WITNESSES AND THE MEDIATOR

A S we continue to seek to agree with all that is moving and active in this dimension, we should be aware of the great cloud of witnesses. In Hebrews 12:23, we are told that these are in the same realm of the Spirit that we have now come to.

> To the general assembly and church of the firstborn who are registered in heaven, to God the Judge of all, to the spirits of just men made perfect.

The term *spirit of just men made perfect* is a reference to the great cloud of witnesses. This term is found in Hebrews 12:1-2.

> Therefore we also, since we are surrounded by so great a cloud of witnesses, let us lay aside every weight, and the sin which so easily ensnares us, and let us run with endurance the race that is set before us, looking unto Jesus, the author

and finisher of our faith, who for the joy that was set before
Him endured the cross, despising the shame, and has sat
down at the right hand of the throne of God.

The great cloud of witnesses are those who have already died and passed into the glory of heaven. Those who lived a life of sacrifice before the Lord are granted a place in heaven as a part of this company called the great cloud of witnesses. We are told we have *come* to them. In other words, they don't necessarily come to where we are, we come to where they are. We step into a spiritual realm, and in this realm they are a part of the activity of this dimension. There are several things we should know about this group that is operating in the Courts of Heaven. First of all, they are those who lived and functioned by faith while in the natural world. Hebrews 11:39 tells us that they through faith have received a good report.

And all these, having obtained a good testimony through
faith, did not receive the promise.

They *obtained a good testimony* means that heaven esteems them. They have gained a place of authority in the Courts of Heaven. Their witness there is paid attention to because they lived a life of faith that caused them to be justified and declared righteous. They have a status in heaven that allows them to petition the Courts. The word *witnesses* has two different ideas attached to it in the Greek. It is the word *martus*. It means "to be judicial and to give testimony." It also means to be a *martyr*. This means that their authority to testify and be heard in the Courts of

Heaven is because they laid down their lives to fulfill God's will. Authority before the Courts of Heaven is gained through giving up our lives for His will to be done. This doesn't mean we have to die physically for Jesus, but it does mean that we must choose His will over our own desires. Based on this definition and description, *not everyone who is a believer and goes to heaven is a part of this group*. We are told in First Corinthians 3:15 that some are saved so as by fire. They didn't lay their life down. However, they did confess Jesus as Messiah. They will not have reward in heaven because it will be burnt up. However, they will be saved.

> **Authority before the Courts of Heaven is gained through giving up our lives for His will to be done.**

If anyone's work is burned, he will suffer loss; but he himself will be saved, yet so as through fire.

This means they spent their earthly life doing their own bidding rather that what God made them for. In the mercy and grace of the Lord they are saved, yet there is no compensation in the next life. This would mean they didn't qualify to be a part of this great cloud of witnesses. This is an elite group that is granted great power because of the life of faith they lived in concert with the purposes of God. Therefore, when they give testimony in the Courts from a legal and judicial place, they are heard. As with all the other aspects of this realm, we are to agree with them. This doesn't mean we have encounters with them, though we can. It means we agree by faith with who they are and what we understand they are doing in that heavenly place. Many times the *intercession* we find ourselves in is because we are picking up what they are presently doing before the Lord. As witnesses before the Lord, they are releasing testimony/intercession there. We are told that the church in earth and those in heaven are still connected in Ephesians 3:14-15.

> *For this reason I bow my knees to the Father of our Lord Jesus Christ, from whom the whole family in heaven and earth is named.*

The saints who are in earth and the ones in heaven are a part of the same family/church. We are vitally connected. Therefore, there are times when the intercession they are yet moving in will empower us. We pick up the passion of their hearts and begin to move in it as well. Revelation 6:9-11 verifies that those who are in heaven are yet praying and interceding.

> *When He opened the fifth seal, I saw under the altar the souls of those who had been slain for the word of God and*

for the testimony which they held. And they cried with a loud voice, saying, "How long, O Lord, holy and true, until You judge and avenge our blood on those who dwell on the earth?" Then a white robe was given to each of them; and it was said to them that they should rest a little while longer, until both the number of their fellow servants and their brethren, who would be killed as they were, was completed.

Even though these are in the heavenly realm, they are waiting for their ultimate reward but are still crying to the Lord for judgments to come from His Throne. There is prayer from those who are in heaven. This is what they are doing as *witnesses*. Their intercession is judicial testimony before the Lord as Judge. We also see that they are those who have been made perfect. They are the *spirits of just men made perfect*. Among other things, this means they are now in perfect union with the Lord. Romans 8:17 tells us that as joint heirs we will be glorified with Him.

And if children, then heirs—heirs of God and joint heirs with Christ, if indeed we suffer with Him, that we may also be glorified together.

The cloud of witnesses is allowed the privilege of partaking of His present-day ministry of intercession with Him. The cloud of witnesses is now able to pray perfect prayers in agreement with Jesus' present-day petitions as the Intercessor. It would seem that those who are in heaven and a part of this group are granted the honor and function of agreeing with Jesus' intercession. We are able also to agree with their intercession. Many times in my prayer time I will pray a prayer something like this: *"Lord, I agree with that which the cloud of witnesses is speaking concerning me. I ask that I might be remembered before You as the cloud of witnesses would speak on my behalf."* I may not completely know what they are saying, but I, by faith, am agreeing with their testimony concerning me.

For instance, a few years ago I had a dream where Ruth Ward Heflin appeared from the cloud of witnesses. For those who may not know who she was in this life, she was a powerful minister who moved in the glory of God. Many would esteem her a mother in the glory movement. I personally never was in a meeting, heard a teaching, or read a book of hers. I only knew of her from a distance. There was no reason in the natural for me to dream of her. In my dream she had come to prophesy over me. When I arrived to where she was, there were those who were trying to interact with her. However, she would pull back. When I came into the room, she fully manifested and revealed herself. I *knew* in the dream that there was something about me that the cloud of witnesses liked. I tell people *jokingly* that I may not have any friends in the earth but I do have some in heaven. As I came to where she was, she began to prophesy over me. As she spoke, someone interrupted her and said, *"But what about us?"* They were asking for a prophecy as well. Ruth Ward Heflin stopped and with a stern look on her face said, *"It's Robert's turn."* I knew she was saying, "He's been left out, fought against, abused, and disregarded, but heaven now declares it's his time."

From that time on, great new opportunities started to happen. Previously closed doors opened. Favor was given. New privileges were extended. This still happens to this day. As a result of this encounter, I began to pray and agree with her prophecy/testimony on my behalf. I began to say before the Lord, "*Your servant Ruth Ward Heflin has declared before Your Courts that it is my turn. I ask on the basis of her testimony that I would be remembered and that new and unimaginable doors of favor and opportunity will now open for me.*" Through this I agreed with and connected to the cloud of witnesses' ministry on my behalf before the Courts of Heaven. Please note that I did not, nor do I, pray to them as saints. I simply acknowledge their activity and ask the Lord to move on my behalf on that basis. They are standing and are regarded in the presence of the Lord. They are functioning as a part of the Counsel of Heaven. We should learn to agree and partner with them as part of the family of God.

We have also come to *Jesus as the Mediator of the New Covenant*. This is according to Hebrews 12:24.

To Jesus the Mediator of the new covenant, and to the blood of sprinkling that speaks better things than that of Abel.

The terms *mediator* and *covenant* are both legal terms. The term *mediator* is the Greek word *mesites*. It means "a go-between, an intercessor, a reconciler." The word *covenant* is about God's irrefutable promises that He has made to us. It is Jesus' past and present-day activities as our Mediator that create this covenant and empower us to experience the benefits of it. Quite often we speak of what Jesus did for us on the cross. This is indeed very important. It is what allowed the verdict and decision to be rendered against the devil and for us. However, Jesus' present-day ministry is very important as well. Without His present-day activities on our behalf, we could not come into what He died for us to have. We would have the promises provided by His death and the New Covenant but be unable to access them. As our Mediator, He is releasing the necessary spiritual activity that allows us to be functionally empowered by what He has done.

> As our Mediator, Jesus is releasing the necessary spiritual activity that allows us to be functionally empowered by what He has done.

I believe that all effective intercession begins with the Lord and in heaven. Revelation 19:10 shows that Jesus is testifying before the Courts of Heaven.

> *And I fell at his feet to worship him. But he said to me, "See that you do not do that! I am your fellow servant, and of your brethren who have the testimony of Jesus. Worship God! For the testimony of Jesus is the spirit of prophecy."*

As John is encountering a heavenly being, he falls to worship him because of the weight of glory he is carrying. He is told not to because of three things. He is a *fellow servant* of John. This would mean he is in human form. He also says he is of *your brethren*. Angels are not our brothers. They are of a totally different dimension and makeup. This would also mean this one speaking to John is in human form. Third, he has the *testimony of Jesus*. Angels do not have the testimony of Jesus as a general rule. This is why when the angel came to Cornelius' house in Acts 10:3-6 he told him to send for Peter.

> *About the ninth hour of the day he saw clearly in a vision an*
> *angel of God coming in and saying to him, "Cornelius!"*
>
> *And when he observed him, he was afraid, and said, "What*
> *is it, lord?"*
>
> *So he said to him, "Your prayers and your alms have come*
> *up for a memorial before God. Now send men to Joppa, and*
> *send for Simon whose surname is Peter. He is lodging with*
> *Simon, a tanner, whose house is by the sea. He will tell you*
> *what you must do."*

Why did the angel not just tell Cornelius and his house about Jesus and the gospel? He couldn't because they don't carry the testimony of Jesus. First Peter 1:12 says the angels want to look into the salvation that has been afforded to man. However, they cannot.

> *To them it was revealed that, not to themselves, but to*
> *us they were ministering the things which now have been*
> *reported to you through those who have preached the gospel*
> *to you by the Holy Spirit sent from heaven—things which*
> *angels desire to look into.*

The angels that fell from their place of abode have no path to redemption. This is because Jesus came as the seed of Abraham and was made like the first man Adam. He did not come as an angel. Therefore, there is no place of repentance for angelic beings that chose to go with lucifer in the great rebellion in heaven. They are sealed in their doom. Jude 6 tells us that the angels who were a part of this rebellion have a certain fate assigned to them.

And the angels who did not keep their proper domain, but left their own abode, He has reserved in everlasting chains under darkness for the judgment of the great day.

This is because they are incapable of salvation. They do not have the testimony of Jesus. These three facts would mean that the being that was helping John was not an angel. This leaves only one alternative. This was one from the great cloud of witnesses. He was on assignment from the Lord to help John understand what was happening.

So what is the *testimony of Jesus?* I believe it is about the salvation that Jesus' work for us has brought. However, the phrase says it is the *testimony of Jesus*, not the *testimony about Jesus*. The testimony of Jesus would speak of that which Jesus Himself is presently testifying. As our Intercessor, Jesus is releasing testimony before the Courts of Heaven. Remember that the cloud of *witnesses* is praying. Clearly their prayer activity in the Courts is considered a *witness* being given before God. Prayer and intercession is a testimony and witness being set forth. Jesus' testimony is intercession on behalf of us. Hebrews 7:25 clearly states that Jesus ever lives to intercede for us.

> *Therefore He is also able to save to the uttermost those who*
> *come to God through Him, since He always lives to make*
> *intercession for them.*

As the Mediator, Jesus is interceding that we might be *saved to the uttermost*. In other words, Jesus is contending for us to fully inherit all that His sacrifice has afforded us. His prayer as our Mediator allows us to possess all that Jesus legally paid for.

Notice as well that the *testimony of Jesus is the spirit of prophecy*. Again I would agree that any real prophetic gift will emphasize who Jesus is, His will, and His desire. However, if we see the *testimony of Jesus* as His present intercession for us, then the *spirit of prophecy* can take on additional ideas. The *spirit of prophecy* can then be seen as a *prophetic unction* that we begin to function from. Whatever Jesus is testifying in the Courts of Heaven through His intercession becomes a *prophetic unction* in the heart and spirit of His intercessors. This is what we are told in Romans 8:26-27. The Holy Spirit empowers our prayers.

> *Likewise the Spirit also helps in our weaknesses. For we*
> *do not know what we should pray for as we ought, but the*
> *Spirit Himself makes intercession for us with groanings which*
> *cannot be uttered. Now He who searches the hearts knows*
> *what the mind of the Spirit is, because He makes intercession*
> *for the saints according to the will of God.*

The Holy Spirit in us makes intercession according to the will of God. In other words, the Spirit takes hold of Jesus' present-day intercession and causes it to be a prophetic unction or the spirit of prophecy we are praying from. This allows us the glorious portion of being a part of the intercessory ministry of Jesus today. This is all the activity of Jesus as the Mediator. He is praying us into and presenting legal ground for our complete breakthrough. We should ask the Lord that the spirit of prophecy would take what Jesus is presently doing and allow us to come into agreement with it. We agree with His present testimony for us.

Chapter 10

THE SPEAKING BLOOD

THE final thing mentioned here is the *blood speaking better things than that of Abel*. To get the full measure of what Jesus' speaking blood does for us, we have to see what Abel's blood produced. Genesis 4:9-12 shows when Cain killed Abel, that Abel's blood cried out.

> Then the Lord said to Cain, "Where is Abel your brother?"
>
> He said, "I do not know. Am I my brother's keeper?"
>
> And He said, "What have you done? The voice of your brother's blood cries out to Me from the ground. So now you are cursed from the earth, which has opened its mouth to receive your brother's blood from your hand. When you till the ground, it shall no longer yield its strength to you. A fugitive and a vagabond you shall be on the earth."

Notice that God is aware that Cain has killed Abel because Abel's blood is crying out. This means that Abel's blood was releasing testimony against Cain. It was asking for retribution and judgment on Cain. On the basis of what Abel's blood was saying,

God passed sentence on Cain. He would become a vagabond and a fugitive. On the other hand, we are told that the *blood of sprinkling* or *Jesus' blood* is speaking *better things*. The blood of Jesus cries for our forgiveness, clemency, redemption, and salvation. Jesus' blood is not asking to be vindicated. His blood is asking that we would be forgiven and given a future. The blood is speaking better things. Notice also that the blood is *speaking*, not having spoken. This means that not only are our past sins forgiven, but for anything that we do now, we can appropriate this blood and come into agreement with its voice. As we repent, we agree with this blood and its voice. Repentance is essential to agreeing with the blood. First John 1:6-7 shows that we must bring things to the light. This means we come out of darkness through repentance.

> *If we say that we have fellowship with Him, and walk in darkness, we lie and do not practice the truth. But if we walk in the light as He is in the light, we have fellowship with one another, and the blood of Jesus Christ His Son cleanses us from all sin.*

Notice that only as we walk in the light as He is in the light does the blood cleanse and keep on cleansing us. Walking in the light does not mean perfect living. Walking in the light means honest living. In other words, I bring hidden things to light through confession and repentance. This is primarily before the Lord, but can involve people in certain situations. When I confess and repent, I have stepped out of darkness and into the light. The blood is now speaking for me and cleansing me from all sin! I have taken advantage of that which is speaking for me and granting God the legal right to forgive me. God's heart has always been to forgive; He just needed the legal right to do it. Jesus' blood granted Him that legal right. When we come out of darkness and into light, the speaking blood now testifies for us. God's passion can now be released concerning us.

> **When we come out of darkness and into light, the speaking blood now testifies for us. God's passion can now be released concerning us.**

The blood of Jesus is one of, if not *the* primary voice we should know how to agree with in the Courts. When we know how to use the blood, we can silence voices that are speaking against us. Isaiah 54:17 states that weapons that have been formed against us cannot prosper if we can silence voices.

> "No weapon formed against you shall prosper,
> And every tongue which rises against you in judgment
> You shall condemn.
> This is the heritage of the servants of the Lord,

And their righteousness is from Me,"
Says the Lord.

Note that the weapons are unable to prosper or be effective against us because the tongue that is driving them is condemned. A weapon can be a curse that is operating against our lives. The real issue isn't the weapon/curse. The real issue is what is allowing it. Any weapon desiring to destroy us must have found a legal right to operate from. This right is always a tongue or voice speaking against us. I have found to not necessarily worry with the weapon as much as the voice that is speaking against me, granting it a legal right. Revelation 12:10-11 gives us major insight into this. We are told about the *accuser of the brethren*.

> *Then I heard a loud voice saying in heaven, "Now salvation, and strength, and the kingdom of our God, and the power of His Christ have come, for the accuser of our brethren, who accused them before our God day and night, has been cast down. And they overcame him by the blood of the Lamb and by the word of their testimony, and they did not love their lives to the death."*

The word *accuser* is the Greek word *katagoros*. It means "one who brings a legal complaint and stands against you in the assembly." This isn't someone in the natural who is angry with you, speaking bad things. This is speaking of the devil and his forces who are concocting evil reports and speaking them perpetually before the Courts of Heaven. These are testimonies designed to resist you and your God-ordained purpose. We get our English word *categorize* from this Greek word *katagoros*. The devil through his persistent attack against you seeks to put you in a box that is not of God's making. The limits on your life are not from the Lord. This is why so many feel as if they cannot get into the destiny and future that the Lord made them for. There are *voices* speaking against you that must be silenced and condemned. The voices themselves have to be judged as illegal and unrighteous and their claim to speak renounced! When this happens, the box or category you have been assigned to by the satanic is broken and you go free.

Two of the main things the accuser seeks to do is fashion the way you see yourself and also the way others see you. Both of these will keep you from your God-ordained destiny. If you see yourself insufficiently, then you will not be motivated to go after the heights you were made for. If others see you incorrectly, they will not extend to you the favor and opportunity that you need to reach the places you were made for. The devil uses voices before the Courts of Heaven to create these concepts in our minds but also the minds of others. The voices before the Courts grant the devil the legal right to actively fashion minds with these ideas. This is why we can be taught forever on identity and who we are in Christ and still never get it. It there is a constant stream of accusations coming against you, regardless of a teaching, you will feel these ways about yourself. You must know how to take the blood of Jesus and overcome through agreeing with its voice and not the voice of the accuser.

The same is true for the way others see you. We must know how to take the blood of Jesus into the Courts of Heaven and silence the voices of the accusers who are seeking to make others believe wrong things. When we repent of anything that the devil might have used to fashion these ideas and then ask for the blood to speak in the Courts, the accuser loses his right to voice these things against us. Our minds become free from shame, guilt, unworthiness, and rejection. We are liberated to believe the right things about ourselves. The minds of others can be free as well, and doors and opportunities can be opened that have been closed until now. This is all because the blood of Jesus is speaking better things than that of Abel. We are learning to agree with the activity that we have been granted entrance into. We are a part of this place and have a divine right to stand in the judicial systems of heaven and see legal rights granted for God's purposes to be fulfilled. What a wonderful place and honor given to us as the saints of God.

> You must know how to take the blood of Jesus and overcome through agreeing with its voice and not the voice of the accuser.

Lord, we come before You as God, the Judge of All. Thank You that You are the Ancient of Days. We honor, worship, and adore You from this place. Would You allow us to present testimony and evidence that will cause decisions to be rendered and breakthroughs to come. Grant us grace that we might stand before You in the favor that has been given to us by the blood of Your Son.

As we stand here, we are aware of the great cloud of witnesses who are here in this place. We choose to partner with them as a part of the church in heaven and in earth. May our partnership allow the will of God to be done. We agree with their testimony before You that we might be remembered and decisions can be rendered for us.

Thank You, Lord, that You are the Mediator of the New Covenant. Thank You that all You have done and are doing is granting us the legal right to possess all that You died for. We agree with Your testimony/intercession through the power of the Holy Spirit. May we set evidence before the Courts of Heaven to see all You sacrificed for be realized.

We come into agreement with the blood of sprinkling that is speaking better things than that of Abel. His blood cried for judgment. Your blood is speaking for forgiveness, redemption, and redeeming of futures. Lord, we repent and come into the light as You are in the light. Let every voice claiming a right against us now be silenced in Jesus' Name, amen!

Chapter 11

BATTLEFIELD OR COURTROOM

AS I began to get a glimpse and revelation of the Courts of Heaven, I began to understand why I had gone through so many attacks. It seemed that the more I prayed and challenged the devil to let go of what he was holding, the worse things got. We call this backlash. As the Courts of Heaven came into view, I recognized that I had for years been inadvertently challenging demonic powers that still claimed legal rights. I began to see that Jesus' manner of contending with the devil and his forces was first courtroom, then battlefield. Of course I had never heard of this before, but I saw it in Revelation 19:11.

Now I saw heaven opened, and behold, a white horse. And He who sat on him was called Faithful and True, and in righteousness He judges and makes war.

Notice that Jesus as the One sitting on the white horse is judging and making war. I began to realize that *"to judge"* speaks of judicial activity while *"making war"* speaks of battlefield. Even

Jesus doesn't march to the battlefield until He has first been in the courtroom. For years, I had practiced what I had been taught. I had functioned in binding and loosing and yelling at the devil and telling him what he wasn't allowed to do. I had seen very little result, but I had suffered quite a bit of backlash against myself and my family. I suddenly realized that if I attack something that still has a legal right to operate, this is what happens. However, I can take the power of darkness to court and ask for a judgment against it and have any rights it is claiming revoked. I can then go to the battlefield and win every time. My whole manner of contending in the spirit world started changing. I began to realize that if there was something that didn't seem to move and/or there was not an answer when I prayed, it was probably because something legal had a claim. We see this in how God led Gideon when He called him to defeat the Midianites. Judges 6:16 chronicles Gideon being called and commissioned to defeat the Midianites who were harassing Israel.

> *And the Lord said to him, "Surely I will be with you, and*
> *you shall defeat the Midianites as one man."*

The Midianites would come and ravage the crops of Israel. Judges 6:1-7 shows the distress Israel was in because of this harassment. The people were impoverished, abused, and bewildered because of the situation.

> *Then the children of Israel did evil in the sight of the Lord.*
> *So the Lord delivered them into the hand of Midian for seven*
> *years, and the hand of Midian prevailed against Israel.*

Because of the Midianites, the children of Israel made for
themselves the dens, the caves, and the strongholds which
are in the mountains. So it was, whenever Israel had sown,
Midianites would come up; also Amalekites and the people
of the East would come up against them. Then they would
encamp against them and destroy the produce of the earth
as far as Gaza, and leave no sustenance for Israel, neither
sheep nor ox nor donkey. For they would come up with their
livestock and their tents, coming in as numerous as locusts;
both they and their camels were without number; and they
would enter the land to destroy it. So Israel was greatly
impoverished because of the Midianites, and the children of
Israel cried out to the Lord.

And it came to pass, when the children of Israel cried out to
the Lord because of the Midianites.

This whole thing began because the children of Israel had
done evil before the Lord. This granted the devil the legal right
to prevail over the people and to steal their crops away. The people cried to God. In this situation, God spoke and sent Gideon to
be the deliverer. However, before he could deliver Israel, he had
to do one strategic thing that was legal in nature. He had to tear
down the altar to Baal that his father was probably the priest of.
Judges 6:25-32 shows this story and what transpired.

Now it came to pass the same night that the Lord said to
him, "Take your father's young bull, the second bull of seven
years old, and tear down the altar of Baal that your father
has, and cut down the wooden image that is beside it; and

build an altar to the Lord your God on top of this rock in the proper arrangement, and take the second bull and offer a burnt sacrifice with the wood of the image which you shall cut down." So Gideon took ten men from among his servants and did as the Lord had said to him. But because he feared his father's household and the men of the city too much to do it by day, he did it by night.

And when the men of the city arose early in the morning, there was the altar of Baal, torn down; and the wooden image that was beside it was cut down, and the second bull was being offered on the altar which had been built. So they said to one another, "Who has done this thing?" And when they had inquired and asked, they said, "Gideon the son of Joash has done this thing." Then the men of the city said to Joash, "Bring out your son, that he may die, because he has torn down the altar of Baal, and because he has cut down the wooden image that was beside it."

But Joash said to all who stood against him, "Would you plead for Baal? Would you save him? Let the one who would plead for him be put to death by morning! If he is a god, let him plead for himself, because his altar has been torn down!" Therefore on that day he called him Jerubbaal, saying, "Let Baal plead against him, because he has torn down his altar."

Before Gideon could march to the battlefield with the strategy of God to defeat the Midianites, he had to tear down this altar. Baal was also one of the gods of Midian. It was impossible for Gideon to go to the battlefield and win while his house was in allegiance with Baal. The principle is, you can never pull down what owns you. This altar that his father tended empowered the demonic. It gave the demonic rights against Gideon and his father's house. The altar had to be removed, the sacrifices silenced, and the gate to the demonic shut so Midian would have no power against Gideon and Israel. Their gods could not help them to defeat an Israel that they no longer owned.

You can never pull down what owns you.

Gideon and some of his companions obeyed the Lord and tore the altar down. This broke the legal claim of the demonic off Israel. When everyone woke up the next day and figured out what had been done, they were furious at Gideon. However, his father defended him. This is significant, because as the priest of this altar, this man would have had an undying allegiance to Baal. However, when the altar was destroyed, his mind was freed from the influence of Baal. So instead of siding with the people, he now defended his son. When powers of darkness come down and their legal rights are revoked, the minds of people go free. This is what we need to see for mass salvations to happen in a culture. Second Corinthians 4:3-4 unveils for us that the reason people reject the good news of the gospel is because powers of darkness are blinding their minds.

> *But even if our gospel is veiled, it is veiled to those who*
> *are perishing, whose minds the god of this age has blinded,*
> *who do not believe, lest the light of the gospel of the glory of*
> *Christ, who is the image of God, should shine on them.*

The god of this age cannot operate unless there is a legal right he is claiming. It can be concerning the sin in the history of a nation for which the ecclesia/church must repent. On a family level, it can be the iniquity and sin in the history of the family that is allowing the god of this age to claim them for himself. Someone in the family must come into the Courts of Heaven and undo the legal claim that is being made to hold them. Once this is legally revoked, people's minds can be free to respond to the good news of who Jesus is and what He has done. The problem is, satan has a legal right to claim the minds. If we are to see these minds freed, the legal right he is using to hold them must be revoked.

This is what happened when the altar of Baal came down. The result was Gideon then marched to the battlefield and routed the enemy. They were defeated and their power over Israel was broken. Before they went to the battlefield, however, the legal right being used had to be annulled, revoked, and renounced. This allowed Gideon and the army to win a great victory according to Judges 7:17-21. They followed the strategy of the Lord in battle and won because the defense of Midian had been taken away in the Courts of Heaven.

*And he said to them, "Look at me and do likewise; watch,
and when I come to the edge of the camp you shall do as I
do: When I blow the trumpet, I and all who are with me,
then you also blow the trumpets on every side of the whole
camp, and say, 'The sword of the Lord and of Gideon!' "*

*So Gideon and the hundred men who were with him came to
the outpost of the camp at the beginning of the middle watch,
just as they had posted the watch; and they blew the trumpets
and broke the pitchers that were in their hands. Then the
three companies blew the trumpets and broke the pitchers—
they held the torches in their left hands and the trumpets in
their right hands for blowing—and they cried, "The sword of
the Lord and of Gideon!" And every man stood in his place
all around the camp; and the whole army ran and cried out
and fled.*

There was a rout and a great defeat of the enemy forces on the
battlefield. If we can break covenants with the devil that are in
our father's house/family lines, his legal rights are removed. We
will then march to the battlefield and win every time. However,
to try to go to the battlefield without judicially dealing with the
issues speaking and empowering the devil will bring defeat and
backlash. May the Lord help us to see success on every level as we
learn to function in the Courts and stand in His presence.

Having pointed out the need to *go to court* to revoke the
legal rights of the devil, we also should know the significance of
winning on the battlefield. Once we have gotten legal things in
place, we can then challenge the powers of darkness within our
jurisdiction. We can see this principle in being *kings and priests*

but also operating as *judges* ourselves. From the king and priest perspective, we function in the Courts as priests. This is what the priests did in the Old Covenant. Their job was through offerings, sacrifice, and intercession to get legal things in place. This is why, for instance, kings would not go to battle until priests had offered sacrifices. We see this in the days when Saul was made king in First Samuel 13:7-14.

Once we have gotten legal things in place, we can then challenge the powers of darkness within our jurisdiction.

And some of the Hebrews crossed over the Jordan to the land of Gad and Gilead.

As for Saul, he was still in Gilgal, and all the people followed him trembling. Then he waited seven days, according to the time set by Samuel. But Samuel did not come to Gilgal; and the people were scattered from him. So Saul said, "Bring a burnt offering and peace offerings here to me." And he offered the burnt offering. Now it happened, as soon as he had finished presenting the burnt offering, that Samuel came; and Saul went out to meet him, that he might greet him.

And Samuel said, "What have you done?"

Saul said, "When I saw that the people were scattered from me, and that you did not come within the days appointed, and that the Philistines gathered together at Michmash, then I said, 'The Philistines will now come down on me at Gilgal, and I have not made supplication to the Lord.' Therefore I felt compelled, and offered a burnt offering."

And Samuel said to Saul, "You have done foolishly. You have not kept the commandment of the Lord your God, which He commanded you. For now the Lord would have established your kingdom over Israel forever. But now your kingdom shall not continue. The Lord has sought for Himself a man after His own heart, and the Lord has commanded him to be commander over His people, because you have not kept what the Lord commanded you."

Samuel had commanded Saul to wait until he came. When Samuel as the priest, and therefore the one who had the right to offer the sacrifice, was delayed, Saul took it upon himself to offer this offering. This was a serious violation. The result was God revoking the initial intent that He had toward Saul. This all happened because Saul as king stepped into the role of priest. This was forbidden in the Old Covenant. There was to be no blurring of the lines between king and priest in the Old Testament. In the New Covenant however, we are both king and priest to our God. Revelation 1:6 tells us that we have been made both kings and priests to our God.

*And has made us kings and priests to His God and Father, to
Him be glory and dominion forever and ever. Amen.*

Through our function as kings and priests, we get legal things
in place but then go to battle as well. Second Samuel 11:1 tells us
that the function of a king is to go to war.

*It happened in the spring of the year, at the time when kings
go out to battle, that David sent Joab and his servants with
him, and all Israel; and they destroyed the people of Ammon
and besieged Rabbah. But David remained at Jerusalem.*

David had become lazy and soft. As a king, he should have
been on the battlefield. This is what the scripture says kings were
to do. The whole point is that we, through our intercession and
function as priests to our God, set legal things in place in the
Courts of Heaven. From this place, we go to war and win victories.

This idea can be seen in us functioning as *judges* in the Courts
of Heaven. In Daniel 7:9-10 when we see the Courts of Heaven
in operation, we see not just one throne or seat but multiples of
them.

*I watched till thrones were put into place,
And the Ancient of Days was seated;
His garment was white as snow,
And the hair of His head was like pure wool.
His throne was a fiery flame,
Its wheels a burning fire;*

A fiery stream issued
And came forth from before Him.
A thousand thousands ministered to Him;
Ten thousand times ten thousand stood before Him.
The court was seated,
And the books were opened.

Multiple thrones are put into place because the Courts of Heaven is a *tribunal court and not a jury court*. In other words, decisions are made in this court from a panel of judges. This is why there were *thrones*, plural, that were set in place. In Isaiah 43:26, we are told that putting God in remembrance is a way we present cases in the Courts of Heaven. However, we are also told that we are to *contend* together with the Lord in this place.

Put Me in remembrance;
Let us contend together;
State your case, that you may be acquitted.

The word *contend* in the Hebrew is *palal*. It means "to judge." The Lord is declaring that He and we together will *judge* anything that would stand against His purposes. When we have gotten legal things in place in the Courts of Heaven through our activities, we can then step into our position as judges and render decrees. These decrees are setting into place the rulings of the Courts of Heaven. We, functioning as judges in the Courts of Heaven, are a part of the process of complete and total victory. We have gained the privilege of not only getting legal things in place but also forcibly executing them into place as a part of the operation of the heavenly realm. We will function as those who judge and make war from a Courts of Heaven perspective. The result will be the annihilation of demonic resistance and the establishment of Jesus' kingdom rule.

Chapter 12

REDEEMING YOUR BLOODLINE:
Sin, Transgression, Deceit, and Iniquity

O NE of the main things the devil as the *antidikos* uses to build cases against us is iniquity. David spoke of this issue in Psalm 32:1-2. He speaks of four different types of trespasses against the Lord. All four can become legal rights the devil can use.

> *Blessed is he whose transgression is forgiven,*
> *Whose sin is covered.*
> *Blessed is the man to whom the Lord does not impute*
> *iniquity,*
> *And in whose spirit there is no deceit.*

David speaks of *sin, transgression, deceit, and iniquity.* Sin means to *fall short* in both the Hebrew and Greek language. This can be morally or ethically not reaching a standard. This is a trespass against the *holiness of God.* This can involve lust, uncleanness, and giving in to the appetites of the flesh. We are told in Romans 3:23 that all have come short of God's glory and standard. This is why we need a Savior.

For all have sinned and fall short of the glory of God.

If we allow ourselves to be given over to the lust of the flesh and the lust of the eyes, satan can have a legal right to build cases against us with this. We must surrender ourselves to the holiness of the Lord and allow His nature to be fully formed in us. When we recognize the efforts of satan to find evidence against us as a legal right, this will cause us to seek to walk in a holy way before the Lord. It isn't the Lord who will do us harm; it is the devil because he has discovered a legal right to bring destruction. If we should sin, this will also cause us to repent quickly. We don't want satan to have something against us that can devour our lives.

The second word that David used was transgression. This is the Hebrew word *pesha*. It means "a revolt, rebellion, to break away from authority, to step across a boundary." This is a trespass against the *authority of God*. As serious as violating the holiness of God is, it would appear in scripture that breaching the authority of God is even more serious. This is probably because this was *the* sin of satan when he was set in heaven as the angel lucifer. His sin was rebellion against God. We see this is Isaiah 14:13-15.

For you have said in your heart:
"I will ascend into heaven,

I will exalt my throne above the stars of God;
I will also sit on the mount of the congregation
On the farthest sides of the north;
I will ascend above the heights of the clouds,
I will be like the Most High."
Yet you shall be brought down to Sheol,
To the lowest depths of the Pit.

The Lord warned lucifer that because of the pride, arrogance, and rebellion that was in his heart, he would be cast down. This was driven by his inability to stay in his place. He always esteemed to have a place that wasn't his. Paul actually warned Timothy about setting people in places of leadership too quickly in First Timothy 3:6. This warning is because they haven't matured enough to handle a place of authority without it causing pride and then rebellion to ensue.

Not a novice, lest being puffed up with pride he fall into the
same condemnation as the devil.

Just like God dealt strongly with satan in heaven when he rebelled, so it seems that our sin against the authority of God receives stricter judgment. Perhaps it is because satan brings cases against us accusing us before the Lord. Perhaps his case is that if he was dealt with so harshly because of his rebellion so must we be as well. We must not allow there to be rebellion in us toward the Lord or toward authority that would represent the Lord. There are clear places in scripture where people rebelled and suffered strong judgments. Of course the whole scenario of

Korah and his rebellion against Moses and God comes up from Numbers 16:23-35. Korah and his company had rebelled against Moses and questioned and fought against his leadership from God. The result was judgment against him.

We must not allow there to be rebellion in us toward the Lord or toward authority that would represent the Lord.

So the Lord spoke to Moses, saying, "Speak to the congregation, saying, 'Get away from the tents of Korah, Dathan, and Abiram.'"

Then Moses rose and went to Dathan and Abiram, and the elders of Israel followed him. And he spoke to the congregation, saying, "Depart now from the tents of these wicked men! Touch nothing of theirs, lest you be consumed in all their sins." So they got away from around the tents of Korah, Dathan, and Abiram; and Dathan and Abiram came out and stood at the door of their tents, with their wives, their sons, and their little children.

*And Moses said: "By this you shall know that the Lord has
sent me to do all these works, for I have not done them of
my own will. If these men die naturally like all men, or if
they are visited by the common fate of all men, then the Lord
has not sent me. But if the Lord creates a new thing, and
the earth opens its mouth and swallows them up with all that
belongs to them, and they go down alive into the pit, then
you will understand that these men have rejected the Lord."*

*Now it came to pass, as he finished speaking all these words,
that the ground split apart under them, and the earth opened
its mouth and swallowed them up, with their households and
all the men with Korah, with all their goods. So they and all
those with them went down alive into the pit; the earth closed
over them, and they perished from among the assembly.
Then all Israel who were around them fled at their cry, for
they said, "Lest the earth swallow us up also!"*

*And a fire came out from the Lord and consumed the two
hundred and fifty men who were offering incense.*

The sin of rebellion against the authority of God resulted in
severe judgment. We must deal with any rebellion in our hearts.
On the basis of God's Word, the devil can take the opportunity
to demand a right to devour. He can come before the Courts of
Heaven and cite God's Word and even past occurrences as a right
to destroy. If we will walk humbly and repent, these rights can and
will be revoked and removed.

The third word is *deceit*. David spoke of there being no deceit
in the spirit. This is the Hebrew word *rmiyah*. It means "treachery,
or to hurl or shoot, to betray." This is a sin against *others*. The first

two sins are against God. This one is a sin that is doing damage to other people in some form or fashion. I have found that sin that inflicted damage on others is greatly used by the devil in the Courts. He claims a legal right to land devouring forces as a result. There are many places in scripture where we see the sin against other people bringing judgment. The Lord declares in Micah 2:1-3 that if someone purposes to steal away what is assigned and designated to another, it will bring devastating consequences.

> *Woe to those who devise iniquity,*
> *And work out evil on their beds!*
> *At morning light they practice it,*
> *Because it is in the power of their hand.*
> *They covet fields and take them by violence,*
> *Also houses, and seize them.*
> *So they oppress a man and his house,*
> *A man and his inheritance.*
>
> *Therefore thus says the Lord:*
>
> *"Behold, against this family I am devising disaster,*
> *From which you cannot remove your necks;*
> *Nor shall you walk haughtily,*
> *For this is an evil time."*

This is speaking of those who have gained authority yet use it to steal, oppress, and abuse others. If they take away a man's inheritance, there will be a disaster devised not just against the one who did it but their family lineage. It is said that there will be no escaping this. Sin against others can be a very powerful thing against people. We must use any authority we have righteously and not oppressively. If we have abused someone, we should repent and seek to bring restitution and restoration. Scriptures such as these are used by the devil to level cases against us when we are guilty. We must repent and ask for forgiveness from God and even others. This is the way we remove the cases that satan would claim to have against us.

> ## We must use any authority we have righteously and not oppressively.

The fourth word that David used was *iniquity*. The word itself in the Hebrew is *avon*. It means "a perversity, crooked, to be twisted." Iniquity is the *history of sin in the bloodline*. This is one of the things satan uses the most effectively in the Courts of Heaven against us. He claims legal cause against us, not just because of our sin, but also the sins of our ancestors. If they have committed sin, transgressions, or deceit, this can be brought up against us as a legal right to land curses and bring devouring forces. We can understand this by looking at a portion of the prayer of Daniel in Daniel 9:16. He was seeking to deal with anything that would delay or deny Israel's release from captivity.

*O Lord, according to all Your righteousness, I pray, let
Your anger and Your fury be turned away from Your city
Jerusalem, Your holy mountain; because for our sins, and for
the iniquities of our fathers, Jerusalem and Your people are a
reproach to all those around us.*

Note that Daniel was not just repenting for his own sins but
also for the *iniquities* of the fathers. They had been in captivity
for almost 70 years. He knew that the legal right claimed by the
enemy to do this to the whole nation was the past sin in the history of the nation. If they were to come out of captivity, these sins
and their legal right had to be dealt with and revoked. Daniel was
repenting for these iniquities. We can see this in a very clear way
in Second Samuel 21:1-3.

*Now there was a famine in the days of David for three years,
year after year; and David inquired of the Lord. And the
Lord answered, "It is because of Saul and his bloodthirsty
house, because he killed the Gibeonites." So the king called
the Gibeonites and spoke to them. Now the Gibeonites
were not of the children of Israel, but of the remnant of
the Amorites; the children of Israel had sworn protection
to them, but Saul had sought to kill them in his zeal for the
children of Israel and Judah.*

*Therefore David said to the Gibeonites, "What shall I do for
you? And with what shall I make atonement, that you may
bless the inheritance of the Lord?"*

The Gibeonites were one of the nations that Joshua and the army of Israel was supposed to have destroyed in their conquest of the Promised Land. However, the Gibeonites had deceived Joshua and the leaders, primarily because they didn't ask counsel of the Lord. Instead of defeating them, they made covenant with them. Even though the covenant was made under false pretenses, as far as God was concerned, it still stood. Generations later, when Saul killed the Gibeonites instead of honoring the covenant, it gave the devil legal cause against Israel. Seventy years later after the fact, there is now a famine in the land for three years. When David decides to ask God *why*, the Lord unveils it is because of what Saul did and his breaking of this covenant. The lack of rain, drought, and famine were a legal result granted to the devil against Israel through this broken covenant. There had been prayer for the land, but no response from heaven. The history of sin was being used to cancel the effects of the prayers. David requested of the Gibeonites what was necessary to see the covenant restored and this curse lifted. They gave him things they desired. David fulfilled them. The Bible then makes a powerful statement in Second Samuel 21:14.

> *They buried the bones of Saul and Jonathan his son in the country of Benjamin in Zelah, in the tomb of Kish his father. So they performed all that the king commanded. And after that God heeded the prayer for the land.*

David showed honor to the house of Saul, while meeting the demands of the Gibeonites. The result of this activity was the legal right satan was claiming, was revoked and the land was blessed again. We must know how to "reach back" into history and deal with any claim the devil has against us. Our ancestors' sins can be silenced so the devil has no right to use them presently against the intentions of God for our lives.

> We must know how to "reach back" into history and deal with any claim the devil has against us.

The New Testament also speaks of the history of sin or iniquity operating against us legally. Jesus, in speaking to the religious leaders of His day in Matthew 23:29-32, warned them against allowing the iniquity in their bloodline to drive them to even further wickedness.

> *Woe to you, scribes and Pharisees, hypocrites! Because you build the tombs of the prophets and adorn the monuments of the righteous, and say, "If we had lived in the days of our fathers, we would not have been partakers with them in the blood of the prophets."*

Therefore you are witnesses against yourselves that you are sons of those who murdered the prophets. Fill up, then, the measure of your fathers' guilt.

In an effort to declare themselves righteous because of their religious activities through building monuments and tombs to prophets and righteous people whom their ancestors killed, Jesus said they were actually releasing a testimony against themselves. They were acknowledging the iniquity in their bloodline of rebellion and sedition against the Lord and His messengers. When Jesus tells them to *"Fill up then the measure of your fathers' guilt,"* He is unveiling that the iniquity in their bloodline will cause them to kill the Son of God. The iniquity in the bloodline had created within them a propensity toward rebellion. This rebellion left them unable to receive Jesus. As a result of their unwillingness to deal with what was working in them and against them, they were destined to do the unthinkable. They would crucify Jesus and fill up the full measure of their sin. This would grant the legal right necessary to see Israel judged and destroyed. The temple would be decimated. This is what Jesus prophesied of in Luke 21:5-6.

Then, as some spoke of the temple, how it was adorned with beautiful stones and donations, He said, "These things which you see—the days will come in which not one stone shall be left upon another that shall not be thrown down."

Jesus was letting them know that because they rejected Him and then killed Him, the judgment against them would be sure. That which they put such confidence and pride in would itself be destroyed. This would be the result of their sin as a people being complete. God spoke to Abraham about this in Genesis 15:12-16. He unveiled to Abraham that after 400 years of captivity and slavery in Egypt, they would return to this land. The reason there had to be four centuries that passed was because God couldn't legally judge the present inhabitants and remove them yet. Their sin was not complete or full.

> *Now when the sun was going down, a deep sleep fell upon Abram; and behold, horror and great darkness fell upon him. Then He said to Abram: "Know certainly that your descendants will be strangers in a land that is not theirs, and will serve them, and they will afflict them four hundred years. And also the nation whom they serve I will judge; afterward they shall come out with great possessions. Now as for you, you shall go to your fathers in peace; you shall be buried at a good old age. But in the fourth generation they shall return here, for the iniquity of the Amorites is not yet complete."*

The Amorites could not be cast from their land until the iniquity gave God the legal right to judge them, remove them, and give the land to Joshua and Israel. Iniquity, or the history of sin in a bloodline, is used legally against us. This is why we must repent of it and ask for the blood of Jesus to speak on our behalf. Otherwise, the devil will build cases against us from these things. There are so many times when people wonder *why* bad and hurtful things are happening to them. They question *why* they can never come into the places they know they are to occupy. These scenarios can be the result of iniquity that is speaking against us in the bloodline. These voices must be silenced. Once these are put to rest and nullified, resistance will stop and blessings previously contended for can come.

First Peter 1:17-19 tells us how we can escape the reach of our ancestors' iniquity. That which would seek to fashion our future is revoked, removed, and silenced.

> *And if you call on the Father, who without partiality judges according to each one's work, conduct yourselves throughout the time of your stay here in fear; knowing that you were not redeemed with corruptible things, like silver or gold, from your aimless conduct received by tradition from your fathers, but with the precious blood of Christ, as of a lamb without blemish and without spot.*

We are told and cautioned that God *judges* without partiality. Therefore, we are to walk in the fear of the Lord. Notice that we are told we have been redeemed by the precious blood of the Lamb. This blood has revoked the reach of the iniquity of our bloodline. This is what is meant by *aimless conduct received by the tradition from your fathers*. In other words, iniquity will create within us propensities and desires that are against the will of God. We must actively take the blood of Jesus and silence the rights that iniquity would claim and the power of the devil associated with it. Remember that in the Courts of Heaven we are putting fully into place the stated verdict of the cross. We answer every claim against us by His blood. We have a right to stand in the Courts of Heaven and declare that we are redeemed by this blood. Therefore, all claims against us are revoked, removed, and erased. They are cancelled according the legal work of Jesus on the cross! We, many times, have to address specific issues in our bloodline. The devil knows we have everything we need at our disposal because of who Jesus is and what He has done for us. However, satan will seek to require us to address certain issues that are specific. He will claim a case against us that denies us our breakthrough, healing, recovery, and destiny. We must actively and aggressively take the blood of Jesus and through repentance use it to silence this voice and claim against us. When we do, this frees us from the claims of iniquity and launches us into our future.

> All claims against us are revoked, removed, and erased. They are cancelled according the legal work of Jesus on the cross!

One of the most significant episodes in dealing with my bloodline happened through a dream I had. Let me first say that I had suffered 20 years of delay. I had very clear words from the Lord concerning what I was made for and what He intended for me to do. In fact, back in 1995 or thereabouts, I had encounter with the Lord where He said to me, *"I will make your name as one of the great men of the earth."* This is from a statement that God made to David in First Chronicles 17:8 when David wanted to build God a house.

> *And I have been with you wherever you have gone, and have cut off all your enemies from before you, and have made you a name like the name of the great men who are on the earth.*

God is telling David that he can't build him a house because he was a man of war. However, his son Solomon would build the house, which is exactly what happened. Yet the Lord had raised David from a place of being unknown as a little shepherd boy to a reigning king. His name is registered with the great men of the earth. The Lord used this scripture, which I didn't even know I knew, to speak to me.

For more than 20 years this word haunted me. When it was spoken, I thought I would see movement toward this becoming a reality. However, anything but that happened. I watched as others were promoted, yet I stayed in the shadows. I saw others' influence grow and increase while I was unseen. The years passed. I got older. My prime time in life seemed to come and go, yet I labored in relative obscurity. I wrestled with this word and lived in frustration. Many were the times when I just wanted to quit and give up on what I knew God had said. Things were promised by many that never materialized. Opportunities and doors that were promised to be made available and opened were forgotten and dismissed. Something seemed to always sabotage any prom-ising movement toward the fulfillment of this word. Much hope deferred began to take hold of my life and create a sick heart. I thought that I must not be who I thought I was.

Then I had this dream. In the dream, there was a present-day judgment against me from a natural court because my great-great-grandfather had injured someone through negligence. I woke from the dream with a terror in my heart. The dream was so real that I thought there was a literal judgment and I was in trouble with the law. I was very frightened that because of this I owed a lot of money and had this judgment against me. When I was fully awake, I realized this was a dream. The effects of it, however, were still deeply in my mind and spirit. I realized that God was unveiling something very significant to me about my bloodline. Then the Lord spoke to me. He said, *"Your ggreat-great-grandfather, through negligence, stole the dreams of someone away. Therefore, the devil has claimed a legal right to steal your dreams away."*

I suddenly knew why there had been such delay concerning the word God had spoken to me. The devil didn't want me to have this realm of influence and be a part of expanding the rule of the kingdom of God. He had found a legal right in my bloodline to deny me the fulfillment of this word! I had to go before the Courts of Heaven and deal with this legal issue through and by the blood of the Lamb. I went to prayer and began to repent for *negligence*. I had no idea what my great-great-grandfather had done. I didn't know who it had been done to. I simply took the knowledge and information I had through the dream and used it. I repented for myself, my bloodline, but specifically for the sin of my grandfather.

Remember, I cannot change the eternal destiny of my great-great-grandfather. However, I can see revoked the legal right the devil would claim to use his sin against me. This is what I did. By faith, I stood before the Courts of Heaven and addressed this issue. I knew that I was dealing with something quite significant and this was destiny altering. I asked for the blood of Jesus to speak on my behalf (see Hebrews 12:24). I asked that the right of the devil to use this against me would be annulled. I asked that this case would be dismissed from the Courts of Heaven and not allowed to be presented again. I felt that all that I asked the Court was granted and a decision was made in my favor.

Up to this point, every opportunity had either fallen through or came to nothing. I had been approached several times about being on different television shows, only to see nothing take place. Suddenly, within a week or less I got a call from one of the highest-ranking Christian TV shows on the air. They asked if I would like to be on the show. I had had previous communications with them before; however, nothing had ever occurred. This time, though, because the legal claims against me were revoked, they had me on. We had a record-breaking response. I've now been on this highly rated show four times. I also have been *given* two shows of my own on different networks. My books are best-selling books. One of the books has sold over a million copies. My influence started growing and has continued. The word that God said to me is definitely on the horizon of being fulfilled. God loves to take nobodies and use them to touch different realms. I am grateful and humbled by what God is allowing me to do. However, none of this would be happening if I hadn't dealt with the legal claim against me allowed by iniquity in my bloodline. I had to stand in the Courts of Heaven and present a case to undo what was speaking against me and the destiny God had purposed for me.

Chapter 13

Statute of Limitations

THERE is one more thing I would like to address about the bloodline issue. We must know that God sets a statute of limitations in regard to what the devil can use. As I first began to teach on the Courts of Heaven and the cleansing of the bloodline, I had been influenced to think that we must deal with our personal bloodlines all the way back to the Garden of Eden and Adam and Eve. I accepted this was correct and taught this for many years. However, I was always bothered by what God had said in Exodus 20:5. The Lord Himself actually put limits on how far iniquity could be allowed to work against someone.

You shall not bow down to them nor serve them. For I, the Lord your God, am a jealous God, visiting the iniquity of the fathers upon the children to the third and fourth generations of those who hate Me.

The devil as a legal being and can only operate within the confines of God's law. He cannot make up his own standards and implement them. He seeks to use the law and Word of the Lord against us and exploit us with it. He does not have the right to use anything past four generations in our bloodline *unless* we grant it to him. In my former days, I would teach people to pray, *"Lord, I open my bloodline up all the way back to Adam and Eve. Anything within it that the devil would use to build a case against me, I ask this to be exposed and revealed."* This sounds really spiritual. It is, in fact, coming from a deep heart before God of not wanting anything hidden. However, when this kind of prayer is prayed, it gives the devil access into things that God's Word says he should have no access to. Some have asked that if this is wrong, then why would seers see things deep in the bloodline past the fourth generation. The answer is simple. When we pray that kind of prayer, the bloodline is opened up, and from their gifting, seers start seeing into these realms. However, the Lord would have this sealed. In a natural court there are times when records are sealed so that no one has access to see a person's history beyond a certain point. This is exactly what this word in Exodus does. Paul addressed this as well in First Timothy 1:4.

> *Nor give heed to fables and endless genealogies, which cause disputes rather than godly edification which is in faith.*

When you look into the Greek, this term *endless genealogies* means "unfinished generations." In other words, Paul was exhorting them not to get caught up in the searching out of bloodline issues, either good or bad. As much as I believe in dealing with the legal claims of the devil connected to our bloodlines, I despise the witch hunts that many people go on. They feel like if they can find that one thing that someone did in their ancestry, everything will change. My experience has been that I deal with my bloodline history by faith. I take Colossians 2:14 and ask that the verdict of the cross be executed on my behalf.

> *Having wiped out the handwriting of requirements that was*
> *against us, which was contrary to us. And He has taken it*
> *out of the way, having nailed it to the cross.*

I ask that any complaint or legal cause satan could be bringing against me would be dismissed based on what Jesus has legally accomplished. I also repent for anything I discern in my bloodline by looking at my parents, siblings, my life, and my children. Within these generations, you will see certain iniquitous patterns. Deal with these before the Courts of Heaven. Then I simply ask that anything else I need to know would be revealed to me prophetically. This has happened through me listening to the Lord and paying attention to dreams and revelations from Him. I have been able to see legal issues removed. Philippians 3:15 is a great scripture regarding looking into our bloodline.

> *Therefore let us, as many as are mature, have this mind; and*
> *if in anything you think otherwise, God will reveal even this*
> *to you.*

We are told that our mind should reflect the maturity we have gained. However, we are also told if there is something we are not aware of or seeing correctly, God will reveal this to us. I claim this over my life in regard to bloodline issues. I basically ask the Lord that if there is anything I still need to deal with that I don't know, He would unveil it to me. This has been a very good scripture to claim and to request for additional revelation to come in this regard.

> **If there is something we are not aware of or seeing correctly, God will reveal this to us.**

However, none of the revelations I have received have gone past the fourth-generation issue. This is one of the things that began to convince me that we were making an error in opening our bloodlines up to Adam and Eve in reference to iniquity. If the enemy is limited to only four generations of iniquity in my bloodline, then I can get things finished. I don't get trapped in the whole business of unfinished genealogies. If satan has access all the way back to Adam and Eve, then it is impossible to get things fully dealt with. However, if it is restricted to four generations, we can and will get the work done and see the enemy lose any legal right he is claiming. We must put into place God's statute of limitations based on Exodus 20:5. When we do, we forbid the enemy the right to use anything past the four-generation mark against us.

We can get issues dealt with and finished from our bloodline and move into the success God has for us.

There is one exception to the rule concerning the four-generation idea that I am espousing. In Deuteronomy 23:2 we are told that if someone is of illegitimate birth there is a curse for ten generations.

> *One of illegitimate birth shall not enter the assembly of the*
> *Lord; even to the tenth generation none of his descendants*
> *shall enter the assembly of the Lord.*

The devil can seek to take advantage of the word and the law of God to exploit us and our descendants with this. Satan could seek to deny someone a place before the Lord because their ancestry had those who were illegitimate. In other words, their father and mother were not married. This needs to be dealt with in most family lines. The first thing that should be stated before the Courts of Heaven is that we are not under the law. Therefore, this ruling would have no bearing on me as a believer. When I came into Christ, I came out from under the law and its restrictions and penalties. Romans 7:4-6 lets us know that when we died with Jesus, we died to the law. The law has no more power over us as believers. Therefore, any case satan would try to bring against us, we can submit before the Courts who Jesus is and what He has done to silence that claim.

> *Therefore, my brethren, you also have become dead to the*
> *law through the body of Christ, that you may be married to*

another—to Him who was raised from the dead, that we should bear fruit to God. For when we were in the flesh, the sinful passions which were aroused by the law were at work in our members to bear fruit to death. But now we have been delivered from the law, having died to what we were held by, so that we should serve in the newness of the Spirit and not in the oldness of the letter.

We also should repent for any illegitimacy in our bloodline. We can ask for the blood of Jesus to speak for us. This is actively putting into place all that Jesus has done for us. We are removing any and all legal arguments that could be used to deny us a place ordained by God.

As important as seeing satan's legal rights revoked that he would claim on the basis of iniquity, there is another issue associated with our bloodlines. This is the covenants that people in our bloodlines have made with demonic powers. Whereas iniquity has a limit of four generations, covenants are perpetual and eternal until someone sees them annulled. We will unveil this in the next chapter.

Lord, as we come before Your Courts, we repent for sin—the trespasses against Your holiness. We repent for transgressions—the trespasses against Your authority. We repent for deceit—the trespasses against other people. We also repent for iniquity—the history of sin in our bloodline. Lord, I ask according to Hebrews 12:24 that Your blood would speak for me as I repent and bring all things to light. I ask that I would be forgiven and any legal right satan is claiming against me would be dismissed and revoked.

I declare Colossians 2:14, that every charge against me is forgiven. You, Lord, took it out of the way and nailed it to Your cross. Thank You that any legal complaint against me is now removed. I ask that any other issue satan could contend against me with would be revealed. Thank You that whatever the legal cause, it will be uncovered so I might know it and repent on behalf of myself and my bloodline. Thank You so much for all that You've done on Your cross that legally answered all complaints. Thank You that the Holy Spirit now helps me as the legal aid to answer all that is necessary to remove what would speak against me.

Lord, I repent for any time I have prayed for my bloodline to be opened up back to Adam and Eve. Forgive me, Lord, for operating erroneously before Your Courts. I ask that any legal right the enemy has claimed based on these prayers would now be revoked. I request that God's statute of limitations now be set in place over my life. That iniquity can only be an issue up to the fourth generation. I ask that anything past this be sealed and not allowed as evidence and testimony before You that would be against me.

I also ask, Lord, that any illegitimacy in my bloodline that satan could claim a right to afflict and deny the promises and purposes of God be cleansed. I would remind this Court that I am free from the mandates of the law because of the death of Jesus. I died with Him and to the law at

His crucifixion. May this be recorded and known before You now. I also repent for any place of sexual uncleanness that resulted in illegitimate births. I ask that the blood of Jesus speak for me. I claim before Your Courts that I am legitimate and have divine purpose. I claim that my family is legitimate and has divine purpose. All other voices that would speak contrary to this are now silenced in Jesus' Name, amen.

Chapter 14

ANNULLING COVENANTS
AND AGREEMENTS

COVENANTS and agreements can be made with the demonic realm. There can be and probably are covenants that were made in our bloodlines that created legal claims against us. The problem is that though there are limits on the effects of iniquity against us, covenants can endure for many more generations. This is because of the nature of a covenant. As far as God is concerned, covenants are perpetual, lifelong, and generational in nature. We can see this from when David and Jonathan made a covenant together in First Samuel 20:13-17. Jonathan so loved David that when he was fleeing for his life from before Saul, Jonathan desired a connection and agreement between them.

> "May the Lord do so and much more to Jonathan. But if
> it pleases my father to do you evil, then I will report it to
> you and send you away, that you may go in safety. And
> the Lord be with you as He has been with my father. And
> you shall not only show me the kindness of the Lord while I

still live, that I may not die; but you shall not cut off your kindness from my house forever, no, not when the Lord has cut off every one of the enemies of David from the face of the earth." So Jonathan made a covenant with the house of David, saying, "Let the Lord require it at the hand of David's enemies."

Now Jonathan again caused David to vow, because he loved him; for he loved him as he loved his own soul.

This covenant was generational in nature. The commitment David made to Jonathan was not just to him for his lifetime. It was also to the house of Jonathan. This is why after Jonathan died, David sought out his descendants that he might bless them. Mephibosheth, the son of Jonathan, was searched for and found in Second Samuel 9:1-3. David then brought him to the king's table and provided for him all the days of his life. This was because of the covenant that had been made with Jonathan.

Now David said, "Is there still anyone who is left of the house of Saul, that I may show him kindness for Jonathan's sake?"

And there was a servant of the house of Saul whose name was Ziba. So when they had called him to David, the king said to him, "Are you Ziba?"

He said, "At your service!"

Then the king said, "Is there not still someone of the house of Saul, to whom I may show the kindness of God?"

And Ziba said to the king, "There is still a son of Jonathan who is lame in his feet."

It was understood that a covenant was something that lasted for generations to come. The devil knows this. Therefore, when someone makes a covenant with demons through sacrifice, those demons claim the lineage of that person. This is intact until it is annulled. This of course is done through repentance and the blood of Jesus.

People make covenants with demon powers for various reasons. Perhaps they needed rain for their crops, or protection from an enemy, or safety for family. Normally the reason behind the covenant was something correct. However, the misguided people made the covenant with powers of darkness rather than the Lord our God. Isaiah 28:14-15 shows the leaders of Israel making a covenant with demon powers. They were putting their confidence in the principalities rather than the Lord Himself.

Therefore hear the word of the Lord, you scornful men,
Who rule this people who are in Jerusalem,
Because you have said, "We have made a covenant with death,
And with Sheol we are in agreement.
When the overflowing scourge passes through,
It will not come to us,
For we have made lies our refuge,
And under falsehood we have hidden ourselves."

This says they had made an agreement with Sheol and with death. This is speaking of the demonic realm. They felt that because of this covenant, when trouble came they would escape. They literally believed the demons they had put their confidence in would be able to protect them and keep them. As crazy as this sounds, this is what people do. I actually had to undo a covenant that someone in my ancestry had made with demon powers. The result of this was immediate freedom from what was devouring my life, family, and ministry. Because I was being used of God and God's intent was to use me in a greater way to expand His kingdom, the devil commissioned a search of my bloodline to see if there was something legal that could be used against me. They found in my bloodline this covenant that had been made generations before. This gave that demonic power the right to afflict me, devour me, and resist God's purposes for me. When I went before the Courts of Heaven and had this covenant annulled, all the attacks stopped. Things began to come to divine order. A restoration process began to recover all that had been stolen. So, in addition to iniquity in the bloodline, we must also ask the Lord to reveal any covenants that are intact with demon powers.

As I have traveled and taught the Courts of Heaven message, I have prayed with many people. I have found those who actually know naturally that a covenant was made with devilish entities. I was in a particular meeting where I led the group in annulling covenants with the demonic. I wasn't aware that there was a lady in the meeting who had been committed to be the *bride of satan*. She had been conceived and raised for this reason by her parents. However, she had had an encounter with the Lord and been saved. The demons would not leave her alone. They would harass, torment, and hurt her in any way possible. I taught, then led the entire group into the Courts of Heaven to ask for covenants to be annulled that satan was using to control people with. This particular lady came to me after the meeting and told me her story. She said she felt a breakthrough come as we stood in the Courts of Heaven and asked for the legal rights satan was claiming to be revoked. I was happy and blessed that she was feeling something had happened. The better part of the story is that she emailed me several weeks later and said that what had happened that night had lasted. She had received permanent relief from the powers that were claiming ownership of her based on covenant. The Lord had rendered a decision on her behalf that had undone the covenant her parents had set in place. The devil's legal right to this lady was annulled and she was freed!

> In addition to iniquity in the bloodline,
> we must also ask the Lord to reveal
> any covenants that are intact
> with demon powers.

I have also prayed with many other people to help them stand in the Courts of Heaven and undo covenants made with demons. I remember one man in Europe who was a very high and respected man in his field and career. However, he battled depression on a huge scale. As we prayed together it was revealed that there had been the sacrifice of children in his bloodline. Please understand, this man had nothing to do with this, but deep in his bloodline there were people who had made agreements with demon powers though the blood of children. Blood is often what is required by demons for covenants to be set in force. Somewhere in his bloodline there had been those who had offered the lives of children to receive demonic empowerment. Therefore, these demons would have claimed this man and his lineage. They said they had the right to afflict him with depression. As we undid these covenants, this man was set free from depression. The legal rights of the devil were revoked and he was freed. So often sicknesses, disease, depression, calamity, premature death, and many other things are the result of covenants with demons. They claim they own the bloodline and the lineage based on the covenant made with them. This must be legally annulled before the Courts of Heaven.

Right after Elisha received the mantle from Elijah, the men of Jericho asked that he would solve the problem of a curse that was in the city. We find this story in Second Kings 2:19-21.

> Then the men of the city said to Elisha, "Please notice, the situation of this city is pleasant, as my lord sees; but the water is bad, and the ground barren."
>
> And he said, "Bring me a new bowl, and put salt in it." So they brought it to him. Then he went out to the source of

*the water, and cast in the salt there, and said, "Thus says
the Lord: 'I have healed this water; from it there shall be no
more death or barrenness.'"*

When we casually read this story, it would appear that the
problem was just some bad-tasting water. However, when we
look deeper we realize something much more sinister and serious was happening. When Elisha speaks the word and heals the
water, he speaks *no more death or barrenness.* In other words, the
problem was not bad-tasting water. The problem was premature
death and barrenness was ruling the city. Even though it was
pleasant and a nice place to live, people died before their time.
The word *death* in the Hebrew is *maveth.* It means "death naturally or violently." The word *barren* is the Hebrew word *shakol.* It
means "to miscarry, suffer abortion, to bereave." In other words,
the problem in this city was children dying prematurely through
natural causes but also violence. Why would this have been?
The reason was Joshua, over 500 years previous, had made an
oath, which created a covenant with demons or gave demons
legal right to destroy. When the children of Israel took the land,
they destroyed Jericho. In Joshua 6:26 we see Joshua having the
people make an oath and swear concerning the rebuilding of
this city.

*Then Joshua charged them at that time, saying, "Cursed
be the man before the Lord who rises up and builds this city
Jericho; he shall lay its foundation with his firstborn, and
with his youngest he shall set up its gates."*

The word *charged* is the Hebrew word *shaba*. "It means to take an oath and to swear by repeating it seven times." It would appear that not only did Joshua do this, but he had the people repeat it also. They made a covenant. The demons took advantage of this covenant. We see in First Kings 16:34 that a man during the wicked reign of Ahab did rebuild the city. Just what was decreed and agreed happened.

> *In his days Hiel of Bethel built Jericho. He laid its foundation with Abiram his firstborn, and with his youngest son Segub he set up its gates, according to the word of the Lord, which He had spoken through Joshua the son of Nun.*

This was the fulfillment of what had been agreed to by covenant through the words and decrees that were made. The problem was demon powers still took advantage of this covenant. The problem still persisted. The decree on the basis of covenant had been that children would die in this city if it was rebuilt. Children were still dying 550 years later because of the curse spoken and set in place by covenant. Elisha undid the curse and set Jericho and its inhabitants free. They were liberated from what had afflicted this city for generations.

Elisha did three basic things to heal the waters and stop the death and bereavement of children. He called for salt in a new bowl. He put it at the source of the water. He made a decree of healing and that no more death and barrenness would occur. These could all be called *prophetic acts*. Prophetic acts can actually be testimony presented in the Courts of Heaven. When we do these things under the leadership of the Holy Spirit, we can be presenting cases in the Courts of Heaven. The new bowl was a declaration that the old was past and they had transitioned into the new. The salt was a statement and request of judgment against the curse that had been operating. The declaration of healing was Elisha operating judicially and setting the judgment being rendered from the Courts of Heaven into place. The waters were healed and a city was freed from the affliction of a 550-year curse.

As we seek to undo and revoke any right of covenant with demons to work against us, we do this through repentance, renouncing, establishing who we belong to, and giving back anything the powers of darkness would claim we have gained through them. Remember that the reason for the covenant that was made was most likely to gain something. Therefore, the ill-advised people of our ancestry would have brought an offering and made a trade with demonic powers. They would have presented something of value on an altar of some kind in exchange for a blessing and empowerment secured. To legally undo this, we must repent, renounce, but also give back anything that has been profited. Otherwise, the demonic power will claim the covenant is still in force. This can be a scary thing. We could have fear that we are going to lose something that we have grown accustomed to. However, we must also realize that all good things come from the Lord. Therefore, anything we would *lose*, the Lord will restore plus more. The reality is that many times the devil will try to convince us that he gave us something that in actuality is a blessing from the Lord. However, we must be willing to pray the prayer and to *give it back* for legal reasons. Here is a prayer for breaking covenants with demon powers from the Courts of Heaven.

As I come and stand before Your Courts, I ask, Lord, that any covenant made with demon powers in my bloodline would be annulled. I clearly state that I do not belong to them. I am bought with the price of Jesus' blood. Therefore, I belong to Jesus. I repent of any activity, offering, trade, or exchange that has been made by those within my bloodline with demon powers. I ask for forgiveness and that Your blood, Jesus, would speak for me and revoke the results of this activity. I renounce any and all allegiance to these powers. I want nothing to do with them. I also give back any benefit they would say I have gained as a result of this covenant. I only want what comes from Jesus and my joining to Him in my life. He alone is my Source, Provider, Protector, Deliverer, and Savior. To Him only is my loyalty, allegiance, and faithfulness. Let every other covenant with the power of darkness now be revoked and annulled in Jesus' Name, amen.

Chapter 15

Jesus Our Advocate

I F we are to see the full effect of the Courts of Heaven operating in our lives, we must understand Jesus' present-day ministry on our behalf. We are told in First John 2:1-2 that Jesus is actively operating and performing as our advocate and intercessor. He is standing for us before the Father, representing our case and claims.

> My little children, these things I write to you, so that you
> may not sin. And if anyone sins, we have an Advocate with
> the Father, Jesus Christ the righteous. And He Himself is the
> propitiation for our sins, and not for ours only but also for
> the whole world.

Not only did Jesus accomplish legal things by His work on the cross, He is now operating from a legal place for us today. The word *advocate* is the Greek word *parakletos*. This is the same word that Jesus used to describe the Holy Spirit as our Helper. This scripture is now saying that Jesus from His heavenly place and function is also operating in this realm. This word means "an intercessor, consoler, attorney, legal aid." Jesus is standing before the Father and representing our cause, case, and claim. He is giving the Father the legal right necessary to allow us to claim all that Jesus died for us to have. His position as Advocate is connected to His place as High Priest, Mediator, and Intercessor. All of these New Testament terms are similar and reflect Jesus' legal work presently for us. As High Priest Jesus is offering and presenting sacrifices that are speaking for us before the Lord. This is His own blood and body. As Mediator, Jesus is removing everything that would keep us separated from God and bringing us to a place of reconciliation. As Intercessor, Jesus is praying prayers that are legal testimony before the Lord. These are cases being presented that give God the legal footing to see His will fulfilled and completed. All of these are very much alike. If we can learn and appreciate all that Jesus is doing for us, we can agree with it and get a great benefit from His present-day activity for us.

> **As Mediator, Jesus is removing everything that would keep us separated from God and bringing us to a place of reconciliation.**

Please note that John defines who the Lord is as our Advocate or attorney before the Father. He is Jesus Christ the righteous. All three of these mean something. They describe the very nature and work of Jesus as One representing us. As *Jesus* His activity is allowing us to experience His salvation. The name Jesus means "to deliver, to rescue." Jesus came to save His people from their sins (see Matthew 1:21). As our advocate before the Father, this is what Jesus' purpose is. He is functioning in this capacity to see us fully delivered, saved, healed, and blessed as the people of God. He is the Mediator of the New Covenant as we saw earlier. His activity is to bring us fully into everything He died for us to have. The word *Christ* means "the anointed One." This can mean not just that Jesus carries an anointing, which He does, but that He is the *appointed One* of God. In other words, He is the One whom God has set and established and will be listened to and regarded before Him. The anointing He carries is the result of the appointing of God. When Jesus stands before the Lord on our behalf, He has the right to do this. He has been chosen and set by God to function in this realm. He carries the anointing and authority of God to stand as our Advocate. He is not seeking to do something not offered and given Him by God. This is why Hebrews 5:4-6 tells us that God Himself gave Him this honor and placement.

And no man takes this honor to himself, but he who is called by God, just as Aaron was.

So also Christ did not glorify Himself to become High Priest, but it was He who said to Him:

"You are My Son,
Today I have begotten You."

As He also says in another place:
"You are a priest forever
According to the order of Melchizedek."

Jesus is the Christ, the Messiah, the One chosen and set by God to operate in the heavens for us. He has been given this place on our behalf. The third thing is, He is *righteous*. Righteousness is what grants authority in the heavenly realm. We can see this in Ezekiel 14:14 where Job, Noah, and Daniel are mentioned. They are said to be righteous, but not have enough righteousness to deliver a nation.

"Even if these three men, Noah, Daniel, and Job, were in it,
they would deliver only themselves by their righteousness,"
says the Lord God.

Their righteousness could deliver themselves individually but would not be sufficient to allow intercession to save a people. This tells us that righteousness is what grants us our position and place in the heavenly realm. In that Jesus Christ is righteous, this says He has the right to speak for us and see God respond. He lived a sinless, perfect life. He was completely obedient to His Father. The result is He has a place with God out of His righteousness that will allow Him to intercede and advocate for us. Whatever He asks the Father, He will receive. When Lazarus had died and was in the tomb, Martha understood this. She actually had an awareness in John 11:22 that God would give Jesus whatever He asked.

> *But even now I know that whatever You ask of God, God*
> *will give You.*

This is a correct assessment of the relationship and authority that Jesus carries with the Father. This is because of His union with God that is absolute and complete. Jesus' full obedience to the Father has allowed Him to have the position He now holds for us.

From this place as we have seen before, Jesus is presenting intercession that is actually testimony before the Lord. This intercession/testimony can be shared with us through the ministry of the Holy Spirit. We get the privilege and right to be a part of Jesus' present-day intercession. As His body, we function with Him as the Head to present cases in the Courts of Heaven. From the unction of intercession through the power of the Holy Spirit, we share in this high and lofty ministry.

The other most important issue I would mention concerning this place and role is that we connect to Jesus' present-day activity for us through our tithe. Hebrews 7:8 shows us that as New Testament believers, when we bring out tithe we are releasing a witness/testimony.

> *Here mortal men receive tithes, but there he receives them,*
> *of whom it is witnessed that he lives.*

The word *witness* is the Greek word *martus*. It means "judicial testimony and report." Therefore, our tithe gives a testimony before the Courts of Heaven. It is speaking on our behalf and declaring that we believe He lives. We are not honoring someone who is dead with our tithe but declaring with the tithe that *He lives.* Even the Old Testament in Deuteronomy 26:14 says they were not to give any part of the tithe to that which was dead.

> *I have not eaten any of it when in mourning, nor have I removed any of it for an unclean use, nor given any of it for the dead. I have obeyed the voice of the Lord my God, and have done according to all that You have commanded me.*

The Old Testament scripture, being prophetic, was declaring that our tithe was to honor Jesus in His alive state as our Inter-cessor, Mediator, High Priest, and Advocate. We were to connect to His present-day ministry through our giving and our tithing. When we release testimony that we believe He lives, we are in fact, connecting to what He is presently doing for us. Our *faith* in His work on the cross and resurrection causes us to be saved. Our *tithe* connects us to what He is now presently doing as our Advo-cate. I can come before Him and actually remind heaven of my tithe. I can ask, on the basis of what it is saying, that the prayers and activity of Jesus for me would accomplish their purpose. I am joined to His life because my tithe is speaking on my behalf!

One other thing I would point out concerning our tithing is that we do it as a part of the Melchizedek order. Many would try to convince us that as New Testament believers we don't need to tithe. This simply isn't true. We *do not* tithe under the Levitical priesthood. We are no longer under this order. We do, however, tithe under the Melchizedek order. This is clear from the scrip-ture we have seen. Therefore, I do not believe as New Testament believers that if we *don't* tithe we are cursed. This was a part of the Levitical order. However, I do believe that if we don't tithe we forfeit a blessing. It is possible to not be cursed, but to neither have a blessing. The issue isn't trying to keep from being cursed. The issue is securing the blessing of a tither. The blessing of a tither from a New Testament perspective is that it is speaking for us and connecting us to His present life. I don't want to miss out on this. I'm not afraid of being cursed. I am concerned with not getting the fullness of blessing that is mine. When we tithe under the Melchizedek order, we have that which is speaking for us. Jesus' present-day prayers are moving on our behalf to see breakthrough come. Here is one true story to emphasize this.

If we don't tithe we forfeit a blessing.

A camp meeting was being held in the interior of Mexico in a desert place. Hundreds came to the meetings. As was customary, a hole would be dug and lined with plastic and filled with water for a baptismal pool. The converts would then be baptized in the course of the meetings. An American evangelist was preaching at the meetings and being translated by the Mexican pastor who was hosting the meetings. The revival had been going for a while.

It was a morning meeting. Everyone was under the tent and in the service. The host pastor had a little boy whom someone was designated to look after. Somehow, the little boy got away from the ones caring for him without being noticed. He fell in the pool prepared for baptism and drowned. He was there long enough before he was found that his body began to bloat in the heat of the sun. When they found him, they went running into the meeting and interrupted the service. Of course the Mexican pastor/father went running and snatched up his dead little boy. There was a shack that was on the property that had walls that you could look through the cracks and into the interior. The pastor ran into this house and shut the door. He began to cradle his dead little boy and cry out in Spanish.

All the people had come out of the tent and were pressing around the shack looking through the cracks as the pastor held and rocked with his little boy and called out in desperation. The American evangelist was one of them who was pressing around the outside of the shack. As the pastor cried out, he ask the people, *"What is he saying, what is he saying?"* They responded that the pastor was saying to God, *"But God, I'm a tither. But God, I'm a tither."* Suddenly, the glory of God filled that shack. The little boy began to spew and sputter. He opened his eyes and began to breathe. His little body shrank back to normal size as God raised him from the dead and gave him back to his father. This happened because this man had a tithe speaking before the Courts of Heaven. It declared that he believed in Jesus who was alive. The life of Jesus entered his little boy and brought him back to life. This is the power of a tithe that witnesses on our behalf before the Lord and His Courts!

Lord, thank You that You are my Advocate before the Father. Whatever You ask of Him, He will do for You. Thank You that You grant me the right to be a part of Your ministry before Him. Thank You that through the Holy Spirit You empower me to partake of this ministry of intercession. Lord, I ask that my tithe and offering would also speak before You and cause You to remember me. Allow my giving to testify that I believe You live. I connect to this life and Your activities from it that are moving for me. Thank You so much. In Jesus' Name, amen.

Chapter 16

THE HOLY SPIRIT:
Our Legal Aid

WE have already established that the Holy Spirit is our *parakletos*. He is our *legal aid* who is helping us maneuver in the Courts of Heaven. This means that He grants us wisdom, knowledge, and understanding that is necessary to present cases and move in this unseen realm. We must learn to pay attention to His guidance and insights. Romans 8:26 lets us again know that the Holy Spirit empowers us to pray effectively. This means that without Him we are most likely just saying words. We need His unction and inspiration to pray efficiently and powerfully.

> *Likewise the Spirit also helps in our weaknesses. For we do not know what we should pray for as we ought, but the Spirit Himself makes intercession for us with groanings which cannot be uttered.*

When it comes to prayer, we have certain weaknesses and limitations connected to our humanity. The Holy Spirit helps us overcome these. As a result of things being legal in the spirit world, it is necessary that we petition correctly and according to protocol. Only through the empowerment of the Holy Spirit can this be done. It is not enough that we have a good heart and wholesome desire. The actual way we present our request is essential to answers coming. This is not because God is seeking to be difficult. It is because we must learn His ways. Psalm 103:7 shows that when we know the ways of God, or how He does things, we can unlock the acts and works of God.

He made known His ways to Moses,
His acts to the children of Israel.

The children of Israel were simply the recipients of the miraculous releases of God. Moses, on the other hand, was instrumental in seeing these miraculous things happen. This was a result of Moses knowing how to partner with the Lord through spiritual activity. Knowing the ways of God and how He does things is necessary to getting our prayers answered. The Holy Spirit helps us in these ways. As our legal aid, He shows us how to make petitions that will allow the Lord as judge to answer and respond to our cry. I was told a true story of a young lawyer who was representing a family in a situation in a natural court. This young lawyer was seeking to make his case before this particular judge. The lawyer went on and on in his presentation. The judge listened patiently for quite a while. Finally, the judge lifted his hand and said, *"Young man, please stop."* The young lawyer ceased what seemed to be endless ramblings. The judge then looked at the young man and said, *"I know what you're trying to do, but you're* going to have to give me a reason." The judge was saying to the young attorney, *"I know and am in agreement with what you are wanting; however, you have not given me the testimony or evidence that will allow me to render that verdict."* This is so often exactly our situation. We have a desire, longing, and cry in our heart, yet we haven't operated according to the protocol of heaven to see the Lord answer our prayers. This is the job of the Holy Spirit in our lives. He is here to help us know how to petition the Lord effectively so that answers might come. Romans 8:22-23 tells us that we have the firstfruits of the Spirit operating with us and in us. The Holy Spirit actually creates groanings that are a part of the intercession necessary for God to answer.

> *For we know that the whole creation groans and labors with birth pangs together until now. Not only that, but we also who have the firstfruits of the Spirit, even we ourselves groan within ourselves, eagerly waiting for the adoption, the redemption of our body.*

There are groanings that are occurring in the earth. Creation and the earth are groaning. We are told that its groaning is associated with its desire to come out of its fallen condition and be freed to its original state. Creation longs for its liberty. In like manner, we who have the Spirit also have a groaning in us. We are groaning to be restored to our eternal and glorious place and position where death has no power over us. This and the redemption of creation will happen at the resurrection of the dead when Jesus comes. Notice, however, that this is connected to the groaning and intercession of the Holy Spirit through us. Sometimes our presentation before the Courts of Heaven is an illogical yet powerful intercession that is born of the Holy Spirit. In these times, we must give place and room for this travail and birth pangs to move in us and through us. Things are being presented and set in order in the spirit world during these moments.

> **We are groaning to be restored to our eternal and glorious place and position where death has no power over us.**

There is no substitute for these groanings that come from the Spirit of the Lord. These groanings and the travail in the Spirit associated with them can accomplish what words never can. These groanings are testimonies before the Lord on our behalf. A breakthrough that I experienced helps illustrate this principle. Several years ago, after planting and having apostolically led a local house, Mary and I clearly felt instructed of the Lord to hand this work off and begin to travel on a kingdom level. This is what we did for over 13 years. This time was very effective and impacting.

About eight years into this time of travel, I had a dream. In the dream the person I had left in charge of the work we had birthed came to me. Before I tell you the rest of the dream, it is necessary that you know this person ended up doing me much harm, damage, and bringing great loss into our lives. It can be very destructive when a person doesn't guard their heart. This one, through selfish ambition and breaking of covenant, spread vicious lies about me in an effort to secure for himself what I had trusted him to steward. This resulted in Mary and me losing what we had labored for and also a great loss of reputation. In the natural, I had no desire or intention to ever return to this local place where all this occurred. However, back to the dream.

In this dream, this person I have spoken of came to me with a legal document in his hand. He desired for me to sign away mine and my children's rights to the city. I awoke from the dream knowing that God was telling me I still had apostolic rights in the city and that I wasn't to give them up. I also know this wasn't about me, but about the generations to come!

I detested this dream. My attitude toward this city was anything but good. After all that had happened there, I had no desire to be back there on any level. However, this dream would not leave me alone. Several years passed. God kept dealing with my heart. The result was that Mary and me made the decision to move back to this particular city and base the ministry from there. We actually started a new local work with our children. This was all a fulfillment of the word of the Lord about the "rights" we had in this particular city. The problem was there was a definite resistance against us in this city. We could never seem to get any momentum. Something always seemed to sabotage it. I knew there were words against me in the spirit realm of the city. I knew the words of people, past and present, were being used by the devil to resist the intentions of God through us. I would go into the Courts of Heaven. I would repent for anything and everything I felt was relevant. This actually had some of the groaning in the Spirit world attached to it. However, nothing seemed to change.

One night in a dream I found myself standing in the "*court*" of this city. The amazing thing was, I had never had an awareness that there was such a place in the spirit realm. I was now standing in a court that I knew ruled and determined what happened in this particular city. As a result of this, I now believe that every city has a "court" that makes judicial decisions in the spirit world about that location. As I'm standing in this court of this city, there is a case against me. It is what is resisting me in this city. There is judicial activity going on about me and my place in this city. Suddenly a young man stands up from the Cloud of Witnesses and gives testimony concerning me. He simply says before this court, "He has a good spirit." On the basis of his testimony, every case against me in this city was dismissed! I knew that what the devil had been using against me was no longer an issue. There was testimony speaking on my behalf before the Courts of this city that had caused indictment against me to be silenced. The result has been that we have seen new levels of breakthrough. Our efforts are now free to produce fruit for the Kingdom of God. There is no longer anything the principalities in this city can use against me.

I remember thinking when the testimony concerning me having a "good spirit" was being announced that this wasn't a very weighty thing. However, the Lord reminded me that when someone is declared to be "good," it is quite a statement. Remember when the young ruler declared that Jesus was "good" in Matthew 19:16-17? Jesus' response was quite startling.

> *Now behold, one came and said to Him, "Good Teacher,*
> *what good thing shall I do that I may have eternal life?" So*
> *He said to him, "Why do you call Me good? No one is good*
> *but One, that is, God. But if you want to enter into life,*
> *keep the commandments."*

Jesus was unveiling a truth that only God in His nature is "good." He was also letting it be known that if He was good, it was because He was God! However, we as the children of God who are partakers of His divine nature can be called "good" as well. When someone is called "good" it is a statement that they possess the nature of God Himself. This is what happens when we are truly born again. We become possessors of His nature. First John 3:9 tells us it is impossible for those who have the nature of God to live in sin and be happy.

> *Whoever has been born of God does not sin, for His seed*
> *remains in him; and he cannot sin, because he has been born*
> *of God.*

God's seed or nature in us will not allow us to be content in sinful living. It will compel us to greater places of holiness because His nature is in us. When the young man in the Cloud of Witnesses made this statement before the Courts, it was all the testimony needed for the Courts to find in my favor. The results have been ongoing breakthrough in the kingdom assignment granted to me and my children within this city.

I have to say that this encounter was preceded by my own repentance, travail, and groaning that I believe was recorded in heaven. This allowed the experience in my dream to happen. My case was brought before the Courts of this city that I might see not only the fullness of my assignment take place, but also to set in motion what God would do for generations to come.

One of the main things I did in this process was to remind God of what He had said. As I prayed before this encounter, I would remind God of His word concerning me and my children. Remember that the word was, "Don't sign away your and your children's rights to this city." I would tell the Lord and remind Him that His word said I had rights in this city. I would petition Him and His Courts on behalf of this for me and my children after me. I would remind the Courts that this was the will and intent of the Lord. This reminding God of what He had said is what I believe allowed the court proceedings I saw and a ruling to take place. The result was the breakthrough I have described that continues until this day. We serve a faithful God and Judge who will vindicate His people before Him!

Chapter 17

The Books of Heaven

AS we learn to present cases in the Courts of Heaven, we must learn to discern what is in the *books of heaven*. The idea of books and/or scrolls is essential to functioning in the Courts of Heaven according to Daniel 7:10. It is no accident that the operation of these Courts is associated with books that are open.

> *A fiery stream issued*
> *And came forth from before Him.*
> *A thousand thousands ministered to Him;*
> *Ten thousand times ten thousand stood before Him.*
> *The court was seated,*
> *And the books were opened.*

The Courts being seated means they have now come to order and are ready to hear cases. The next thing that occurs is books are opened. This is because the cases that are to be heard are coming from these books. This means that cases that the court hears must originate from heaven. Cases that are heard and decided on in heaven do not start in earth. They start in heaven. This requires that someone from earth be able to discern what is in the books that are in heaven. This requires that we be a prophetic people. Isaiah 29:10-12 shows that prophets and seers are those who can discern what is in books from heaven. If books are not opened, then prophetic people cannot understand, no matter how significant their gifting.

> *For the Lord has poured out on you*
> *The spirit of deep sleep,*
> *And has closed your eyes, namely, the prophets;*
> *And He has covered your heads, namely, the seers.*
>
> *The whole vision has become to you like the words of a book that is sealed, which men deliver to one who is literate, saying, "Read this, please."*
>
> *And he says, "I cannot, for it is sealed."*
>
> *Then the book is delivered to one who is illiterate, saying, "Read this, please."*
>
> *And he says, "I am not literate."*

Being literate or illiterate simply speaks of the gifting a prophetic person would carry or not. The bottom line is that regardless of gifting, if books are not open, there is no revelation. This would mean that cases could not be presented in the Courts of Heaven. This is why John wept in Revelation 5:1-5 when he felt there was no one worthy to open the books. This means that not just anyone can open books. They must be esteemed in heaven. This can be the reason why sometimes Courtroom activity doesn't seem to work.

The Courts can only operate from opened books. However, there must be those esteemed and honored by heaven to open the books.

> **Not just anyone can open books.
> They must be esteemed in heaven.**

And I saw in the right hand of Him who sat on the throne a scroll written inside and on the back, sealed with seven seals. Then I saw a strong angel proclaiming with a loud voice, "Who is worthy to open the scroll and to loose its seals?" And no one in heaven or on the earth or under the earth was able to open the scroll, or to look at it.

So I wept much, because no one was found worthy to open and read the scroll, or to look at it. But one of the elders said to me, "Do not weep. Behold, the Lion of the tribe of Judah, the Root of David, has prevailed to open the scroll and to loose its seven seals."

Obviously, Jesus as the Lion of Judah has the right to open books. However, the principle is still valid—we must qualify to be able to open books and therefore present cases from them prophetically. Each one of us has a book in heaven with our prophetic destiny in it—in other words, why we are alive in the earth and what our ultimate reason is for being here. This is seen in Psalm 139:15-16 where David speaks of that which is in the book of heaven.

> My frame was not hidden from You,
> When I was made in secret,
> And skillfully wrought in the lowest parts of the earth.
> Your eyes saw my substance, being yet unformed.
> And in Your book they all were written,
> The days fashioned for me,
> When as yet there were none of them.

David refers to this book as *Your* book. In other words, this is God's book. That means it's about His purposes in the earth. We are here to fulfill His kingdom mandates. Everybody in the earth has something written in His book. We are all born with a kingdom reason for existence ordained before the beginning of time. It is our job to discover this mandate and seek to fulfill it through His empowerment. Second Timothy 1:9 clearly shows that things were set in place before anything ever existed as we know it.

> Who has saved us and called us with a holy calling, not
> according to our works, but according to His own purpose
> and grace which was given to us in Christ Jesus before
> time began.

Notice that according to His purpose and grace things were set in place for us before time began. This means that before there was sun, moon, stars, and anything we know about life in the universe, God ordained things concerning us. He *gave us* purpose and grace. Purpose is what is written in the book, while grace is the empowerment to fulfill it. Purpose and grace are not something He presently gives us or will give us. It is that which has already been given. This means that purpose and destiny are not something we create, but something we discover. We are here to discern what is in the book and the grace associated with it. Whatever our purpose is, there will be grace attached to it. Otherwise, it's not our purpose. Grace attached to it will cause us to desire it, be good at it, and have success doing it. It is that which God made us for.

Another thing about the book is not only is it His book, but He *saw*. What is in this book is what God *saw* about us. Before time began, God looked into the future and *saw* what would be. He sees the end from the beginning according to Isaiah 46:9-10. God declares things that are yet to be seen in the natural.

> *Remember the former things of old,*
> *For I am God, and there is no other;*
> *I am God, and there is none like Me,*
> *Declaring the end from the beginning,*
> *And from ancient times things that are not yet done,*
> *Saying, "My counsel shall stand,*
> *And I will do all My pleasure."*

God had a plan for the future even from ancient times. He declared things that were to happen there. He saw the things that would be necessary for the fulfillment of His plan. Some of those things were you and me. God thought up and dreamed of you and me to meet a need that would be associated with His plan. He purposed the time we would be born in, the task we would fulfill, and the problem we would solve. He apportioned grace to us to accomplish all this. This is what He saw. It was written in a book. What God saw is what determines our destiny and future. We are here as a fulfillment of our seeing God.

We are also told that *my substance* was written in the book. My substance speaks of my DNA. It is what determines not just my looks but my interests, desires, gifts, and propensities. God created me with these that I might gravitate toward what I'm here to accomplish. One of the things we should pay attention to as we seek to discern what is in the book is our desires. Our desires in a redeemed state will be consistent with what is written in the book. These desires are designed to drive us and lead us to what we are to accomplish. So many people believe that God will *make* them do something they don't like or want to do. Nothing could be further from the truth. The Lord actually built us and made us with that which will propel us to what we are meant to be and do. The greatest fulfillment in life will be found in accomplishing what was written in the book that is in heaven. Should we not desire what is written in our book, God will work it into our heart as we yield to Him. There are occasions when someone doesn't want to do something they were made for because they haven't yet surrendered themselves to the Lord. However, when we submit ourselves to Him, according to Philippians 2:13, He produces in us the right desires.

> ## The greatest fulfillment in life will be found in accomplishing what was written in the book that is in heaven.

For it is God who works in you both to will and to do for His good pleasure.

The Lord is very capable of changing our heart and longings to agree with what He purposed us to do. This is actually what happened to me. I did not wish to be in ministry. It wasn't what I desired. Yet when I surrendered myself to the Lord, these supernatural longings began to arise. The very thing I didn't want to do, I began with a passion to desire. I started asking the Lord to allow me to do this thing. This was because God changed my heart when I surrendered. This is because my substance or the thing that would compel me to do His will was written in the book in heaven. The other thing in this book is my *days yet unfashioned*. This means how long I will live and what I should accomplish. We are told in Ephesians 2:10 that certain works have been committed to me for my life and times. They were planned out for me before time began.

*For we are His workmanship, created in Christ Jesus for
good works, which God prepared beforehand that we should
walk in them.*

As the workmanship of God, I was made to accomplish certain
works. This means I should use my life wisely and the time I have
been given in this life. There are things that have been assigned
to me from my book that I am to see fulfilled. We all have a certain amount of time allotted to us. We must use it to fulfill what
is written in the book in heaven about us. When we stand before
the Lord in judgment, our evaluation will be on how much of my
book I fulfilled. Did I do what I was sent and positioned in the
earth to do? This will be the question. Even Jesus had a book that
He was to complete in His earthly life. Hebrews 10:5-7 tells us
that the passion of the Lord was to satisfy what had been written
in His book.

Therefore, when He came into the world, He said:
"Sacrifice and offering You did not desire,
But a body You have prepared for Me.
In burnt offerings and sacrifices for sin
You had no pleasure.
Then I said, 'Behold, I have come—
In the volume of the book it is written of Me—
To do Your will, O God.'"

Jesus said the body He was provided was so it could be sacrificed as a fulfillment of all the bulls and goats that had been
offered throughout the millennia. Everything they had prophesied

of Jesus' body on the cross was fulfilled. However, His body was also so He could live in the earth and fulfill what was written in the book of heaven. Jesus clearly said He had a body prepared for Him that He might *do Your will, O God*. This is the reason for our body as well. We have been granted a body to live in the earth so that we might fulfill what is written about us in heaven. We must steward our body and our time here so that we might be found faithful to what was written about us. First Peter 4:1-2 exhorts us to use our time wisely. We are to use it to complete the will of God appointed to us.

> *Therefore, since Christ suffered for us in the flesh, arm yourselves also with the same mind, for he who has suffered in the flesh has ceased from sin, that he no longer should live the rest of his time in the flesh for the lusts of men, but for the will of God.*

We are to have the correct mindset toward life and its purpose. Notice that suffering in the flesh is when we say no to sin and yes to the will of God. As we do this, we are using our time here to do God's will and not pursue the lust of the flesh. This will allow us to complete what is written about us in heaven.

The devil does not want us to live out what is written about us in the books of heaven. This is because whatever is written about us in heaven is connected to the overall purposes of God. If he can stop us from getting what is written about us in heaven, he can frustrate at least a portion of God's plan. This is what he sought to do with Peter in Luke 22:31-32.

And the Lord said, "Simon, Simon! Indeed, Satan has asked
for you, that he may sift you as wheat. But I have prayed
for you, that your faith should not fail; and when you have
returned to Me, strengthen your brethren."

The words *asked for* are the Greek word *exaiteomai*. It literally
means to *demand for trial*. Satan has an understanding of what
God intends to do with and through Peter. He has an awareness
of what is written in the book concerning him. His strategy to
stop this is to bring Peter to trial in the Courts of Heaven. This is
one of the main reasons for judicial activity in heaven. It is to stop
us legally from fulfilling what is written of us. Satan is claiming
that he has a case against Peter that will deny him the right to
have what is written about him. However, Jesus declares that He
had prayed for Peter. Jesus had stepped into the Courts of Heaven
and had undone the case against Peter. He assured Peter that the
victory was won and he would get what was written in his book.
This indeed did happen. Peter changed the course of history.
He was dynamically used of God. His life did massive damage to
the purposes of the powers of darkness. Satan tried to stop this
through legal wrangling in the Courts of Heaven. However, Jesus
pled Peter's case and won.

It is important to know that Jesus did this as a mortal man and
not as God. This was not a result of some special place Jesus had
with God because He was God. He did not do this as God but as
a man filled with God. If He did this as God, then we are out of
luck. This would mean the Courts of Heaven is off-limits to us.
We are not God. If He did it as a man filled with God through
the power of the Holy Spirit, then it is accessible to us as well.

This is in fact what occurred. Just like Jesus stood and pled the case of Peter, so we too can stand in the Courts and plead our case and even the cases of others. We can request a fulfillment of what is written in our books. We can answer the accusations that would come and see them dismissed. We can win the case and see the purposes of God within the books of heaven satisfied. Peter still went through a time of testing even after Jesus won the case in the Courts of Heaven. He would still deny the Lord and struggle with faithfulness. Yet when it was all said and done, Peter would fulfill what had been assigned and ordained for him. Jesus' activity in the Courts of Heaven on his behalf secured the ultimate victory even though there were struggles to get there. We must know that just because decisions have been rendered in the Courts of Heaven, it doesn't mean there will be no more fights. It simply means the victory will be sure. The legal rights of the devil have been revoked and the right to have what is in the books is secured!

> Just because decisions have been rendered in the Courts of Heaven, it doesn't mean there will be no more fights. It simply means the victory will be sure.

As we stand before Your Courts, Lord, we petition You on the basis of what is written in our books. May we be found worthy to see the book open and to discern prophetically what is written about us. We request before You that Your divine purpose be fulfilled concerning us. May every legal complaint against us from the adversary be revoked, silenced, and annulled. May we see the fulfillment of all that is written in the book become reality. We ask that Your blood would speak for us and we would be qualified not only to perceive what is in the book but to see it come to pass. In Jesus' Name, amen.

Chapter 18

ACCESSING THE
COURTS BY FAITH

MANY people struggle with functionally operating in the Courts of Heaven. They think they have to be some special person with special prophetic gifting. This is not true. After years of teaching and functioning in the Courts of Heaven, I have come to the conclusion that operating in the Courts of Heaven is for everyone, regardless of their prophetic strength or gifting. It is true that certain gifted people can help, but they are not necessary. In some of my earlier books, I inadvertently gave the idea that someone needed a *seer gift* to be able to function on a high level before the Courts of Heaven. I no longer believe this. This would put many people at a disadvantage and would exalt the *seeing gift* to a level of importance that is not good. Anything that makes us dependent for our breakthrough on a certain person or people is not spiritually healthy. Believing and learning that God has made each of us with the capabilities that we need for our breakthrough is essential. If I think that I need someone else other than Jesus to help me find my miracle then I have the wrong perspective. I probably have developed a spiritual laziness that I need to overcome to be able to function in the

Courts of Heaven. I could have just concluded that it is beyond me and therefore I need someone to do it for me. I do believe that it can be helpful for people to agree together. Obviously this is biblical. Matthew 18:19 clearly tell us that there is power in us joining our hearts and faith with others.

> *Again I say to you that if two of you agree on earth*
> *concerning anything that they ask, it will be done for them by*
> *My Father in heaven.*

We can and should be a part of joining with others in prayer. However, when I believe that there is something I cannot access without a given kind of person, this is wrong thinking. I have concluded that if there is something off-limits to me because I don't have access to a prophetically gifted person, this would be unfair. Either the blood of Jesus makes these realms accessible or it doesn't. I am certain that it does. We all can by faith step into the Courts and have audience before the Judge of All.

> **Either the blood of Jesus makes these**
> **realms accessible or it doesn't.**
> **I am certain that it does.**

As I looked and considered this whole scenario, I found something else very interesting. As much as I was impressed initially with these high-powered seer gifts, I discovered I got *more breakthrough* doing things by faith. To me this is the acid test. Does anything change in the natural realm from what we are doing in the spiritual realm? I watched as these seer gifts saw angels, the cloud of witnesses, and other heavenly action taking place in connection to Courtroom operation. The problem was nothing changed after it was all over. I knew something wasn't working correctly. I started just doing things by faith in the Courts of Heaven. To my amazement, breakthroughs came. I was getting more substantial results through doing things out of faith than what all the high-powered prophetic people were able to bring. Let me be clear here. I am not against seers, prophetic people, and their operation. They are a needed part of the body of Christ. I just believe we tend to exalt them out of measure at times. Instead of spending time developing our own relationship and abilities in the Lord, we run to these. This can never take the place of our own operation by faith before the Lord.

So what is the secret to functioning before the Courts of Heaven and seeing prayers answered and results revealed? I want to give us some ideas. The first thing is that nothing can replace a history with God. Many people want to approach the Courts of Heaven as a new, novel way of praying that magically gets results. This idea will backfire on us and not produce what we are looking for. As Jesus taught on prayer in a judicial system in Luke 18:1-8, He unveiled a secret to getting decisions rendered for us. In particular in verses 6-8 Jesus makes statements that show a powerful truth we must embrace.

Then the Lord said, "Hear what the unjust judge said. And shall God not avenge His own elect who cry out day and night to Him, though He bears long with them? I tell you that He will avenge them speedily. Nevertheless, when the Son of Man comes, will He really find faith on the earth?"

Jesus says that God as the ultimate Judge of all the earth would render decisions for His *elect*. We've already seen this earlier. However, it bears repeating. The Courts of Heaven is for us as His believers. It is the place where we find relief from demonic assault based on legal claims of the devil. This Court is designed to take satan and his forces before the bench of heaven and see all Jesus has done set in place against them. We are the elect and chosen of God. Notice that these elect *cry out day and night*. This means they have the history with God I have spoken of. They are not approaching the Courts of Heaven with the idea that it's a formula or method they can get breakthrough from. They have a habitual life of prayer that grants them status in the heavenlies. They cry out day and night! The truth is that most people do not have this. David said before the Lord in Psalm 5:1-3 that his voice would perpetually be heard before the Lord in the morning.

Give ear to my words, O Lord,
Consider my meditation.
Give heed to the voice of my cry,
My King and my God,
For to You I will pray.
My voice You shall hear in the morning, O Lord;

In the morning I will direct it to You,
And I will look up.

David made a commitment to the Lord that every morning his voice would be heard before the Lord. Notice that he would *look up*. There is something that allows faith to arise when we habitually come before the Lord day and night. There is an igniting of faith that will stir in our heart. Plus it gives us a history with God. God knows our voice. David declared that his voice would be heard before the Lord. There are two words that characterized David's voice as he cried out to the Lord in the morning. First David said *give ear to my words*. This word *word* in the Hebrew is *emer*. It means "something said, an answer." David is saying that as his voice is heard before the Lord, it will be him *answering the Lord*. We must understand that prayer is our response to the moving of the Spirit of the Lord. When I pray, I depend on the unction of the Holy Spirit. I am praying out of His strength and power. If we think that prayer is something we initiate, then we have yet to understand the power of it. Real prayer is that which is moving through us by the Spirit of God. We are *answering* with our words that which heaven is originating. This is what makes prayer so rewarding and significant. The other word that David spoke of was *meditation*. It is the Hebrew word *hagiyg*. It means "to murmur, a musing." This is same word that is used in Joshua 1:8 when God told Joshua he should *meditate* on the law of the Lord day and night.

This Book of the Law shall not depart from your mouth, but
you shall meditate in it day and night, that you may observe

to do according to all that is written in it. For then you will
make your way prosperous, and then you will have good
success.

He was to speak the word of God over his life day and night. He was to *murmur it to himself.* This is the only place we're given the right to murmur. We get to murmur the Word of the Lord to ourselves and to God. When we do this, we are developing a history with God. Our voice is being heard in heaven. We are meeting the criteria that Jesus laid out for the elect. We are crying out to the Lord day and night.

The scripture in Luke says that if we cry to Him day and night as the Judge, *He will avenge us speedily.* Quick and speedy decisions are made in our favor when we have a status with God because our voice has been heard. We must develop this place with the Lord. We must by faith spend time in His presence and allow our words to be heard as we answer the moving of the Spirit of God and murmur back His word over us. The thing that got my attention concerning the Courts of Heaven was how quick the answer came. Years of praying had caused nothing to occur. As I shared previously, however, when I stepped by faith into the Courts of Heaven under the leading of the Holy Spirit, an immediate breakthrough occurred. I asked someone who had an awareness of the Courts of Heaven why this happened to me and others seemed to struggle to get answers even from the Courts. Their response to me was revealing. They said, *"Because you had done the work."* I considered their response and thought this is exactly what Jesus said. If we have cried to Him day and night, we have spent time in His presence *doing the work.* There is no substitute for this. I do not want this to discourage anyone who perhaps hasn't been faithful to do this. My admonition would be to start now. God will honor your faith, your obedience, and your commitment. He will see from heaven and reward you openly. This is the promise of His Word.

> ## There is no substitute for *doing the work.*

When I speak of doing things by *faith* in the Courts of Heaven, what I mean is I take God at His word. I see in the Word of God the places, principles, and practices connected to the Courts of Heaven. Therefore, I set my heart and movements to step into these. I trust that as I move the Holy Spirit is going to help my weaknesses. This is what He has promised to do. This is what has perpetually and consistently been my experience. When I am uncertain and even afraid, the Holy Spirit has come to my rescue and empowered me. The Lord loves when we put our confidence in Him in our places of weakness. As we by faith step into these places, we must know that we are *more prophetic than we might have imagined.* Sometimes we glamorize these prophetically gifted people. We almost deify them as if they are not human. The truth is they are very much flesh and blood. We must know though that to compare ourselves to them and their gifting doesn't work anything good into us. Second Corinthians 10:12 tells us not to do this!

> *For we dare not class ourselves or compare ourselves with those who commend themselves. But they, measuring themselves by themselves, and comparing themselves among themselves, are not wise.*

If we allow ourselves to get pulled into this whole scenario of seeking to be the greatest, it doesn't produce anything good. We are not to be measuring ourselves by the gift someone else carries. We are to be thankful for the gifts we have and develop and use them. This is what I have come to be aware of. I don't need to be someone else. I need to be Robert Henderson and release the gifting that God gave me. This is what will build up the body of Christ and make room for me. It is true for you as well. Quit trying to be what someone else is and be freed to be you. There are gifts in you that are necessary to your future and to bless others. Quit being so impressed with what someone else is that you can't see who you are!

With this said, we should realize that if the Holy Spirit dwells in us, we have a prophetic nature. This is because the Holy Spirit by nature is prophetic. John 16:13 tells us that the Holy Spirit will speak what He hears and tell us prophetically what is coming.

> *However, when He, the Spirit of truth, has come, He will guide you into all truth; for He will not speak on His own*

authority, but whatever He hears He will speak; and He will
tell you things to come.

This scripture lets us know that the Holy Spirit will create
within us a prophetic nature and abilities. If we have the Spirit
dwelling in us, that means we have prophetic capabilities. One of
the reasons we don't operate in these realms is because we haven't
taken the time and effort to develop them. Any gift we receive is
in seed form. It is up to us to cultivate, grow, and steward it into
greatness. Hebrews 5:14 tells us that we have spiritual *senses* just
like we have natural senses. We have to learn to use them so that
we can function effectively in the spirit world.

But solid food belongs to those who are of full age, that is,
those who by reason of use have their senses exercised to
discern both good and evil.

The senses spoken of here are prophetic abilities. Just like
we have fives natural senses of touch, taste, smell, hearing, and
sight, we also have at least five correlating spiritual senses. We
use our natural senses to function in the natural world. We are to
use these spiritual senses to function in the unseen world. This is
imperative as we seek to function in the Courts of Heaven. We
should be open to operating in *all* these senses. One or two may be
stronger than the others, but all are for us. For instance, I tend to
feel (touch) and hear more than the other three. I definitely see
at times and have smelled and tasted as well. When I am seeking
to operate in the Courts of Heaven, I open myself by faith to these
awarenesses. I pay attention to thoughts that come into my spirit/

brain. I pay attention to images that might develop in my mind. I pay attention to the way I am feeling and the words those feelings produce. I pay attention even to smells that are not connected to my surroundings. I pay attention even to tastes that I would have in my mouth. These can all be impressions from the Holy Spirit and help us maneuver in the spirit world, but especially the Courts of Heaven.

> ### Spiritual senses are developed through the effort of using them.

Notice that these are developed through the effort of using them. This is where we must shake free from spiritual laziness and even lies we have believed. The devil tries to come and plant lies in your heart that you can't do this. If that were true then the Word of God is not true. We have received the Spirit of the Lord and have an anointing. This will empower us to navigate in the unseen realm of the Courts of Heaven. I may not *visit heaven*. I may not *see angels*. I may not encounter the *cloud of witnesses*. However, I can take the gifts given me and the grace of God associated with them and operate in the Courts of Heaven. I can present cases in the Courts and see breakthroughs come. All that Jesus has done and is doing is working on my behalf. The Holy Spirit is helping me. I have been granted entrance into His Courts by His blood. I refuse to allow the lies of the devil keep me away from a place that is rightfully mine. I want to encourage you to do the same. Let faith arise in your heart. All that you need, you already have. Believe it and step into the Courts of Heaven and present your case!

As I come and stand before Your Courts, Lord, I ask that I might move by faith before You. I ask for the help of the Holy Spirit to empower me as I present my case before You. You are no respecter of persons. You do not show partiality. Whoever works righteousness and sets their heart to do Your will, You, Lord, will receive. Thank You for helping me in my weakness as I present my case before You by faith. I take up my place granted me by the blood of Jesus. In Jesus' Name, amen.

Chapter 19

PARTNERING WITH GOD IN THE COURTS OF HEAVEN

THE Lord *needs us*. This might seem like a prideful or arrogant statement, but it is true. Just like Jesus in Matthew 21:2-3 sent His disciples to go and get the donkey that He *needed* to ride into Jerusalem, so God *needs* us.

> *Saying to them, "Go into the village opposite you, and immediately you will find a donkey tied, and a colt with her. Loose them and bring them to Me. And if anyone says anything to you, you shall say, 'The Lord has need of them,' and immediately he will send them."*

Jesus had to ride on a donkey into Jerusalem to fulfill the prophetic word. In Zechariah 9:9, the prophet had spoken that the King/Messiah would come in a lowly form riding on a donkey.

> *Rejoice greatly, O daughter of Zion!*
> *Shout, O daughter of Jerusalem!*

Behold, your King is coming to you;
He is just and having salvation,
Lowly and riding on a donkey,
A colt, the foal of a donkey.

Jesus sending His disciples was Him allowing them to have a part in the fulfillment of this prophetic word. There are many prophetic things that are to be fulfilled. God need us to be a part of this process. Acts 3:19-21 tells us that there must be a restoration of all things. For this to occur, God has to have a people to partner with.

Repent therefore and be converted, that your sins may be
blotted out, so that times of refreshing may come from the
presence of the Lord, and that He may send Jesus Christ,
who was preached to you before, whom heaven must receive
until the times of restoration of all things, which God has
spoken by the mouth of all His holy prophets since the world
began.

Heaven is holding Jesus until the times of restoration that the prophets spoke about. This means that the prophetic word must come to pass. God has to have a people to operate with to see this occur. At least a part of this prophetic fulfillment depends on our operation in the Courts of Heaven. We see this in Isaiah 43:25-28, where literally the destiny of a nation is hanging in the balance because God's people have forfeited their rights in the Courts.

I, even I, am He who blots out your transgressions for My
own sake;
And I will not remember your sins.
Put Me in remembrance;
Let us contend together;
State your case, that you may be acquitted.
Your first father sinned,
And your mediators have transgressed against Me.
Therefore I will profane the princes of the sanctuary;
I will give Jacob to the curse,
And Israel to reproaches.

Notice that Jacob is given to the *curse* while Israel is given over to *reproaches*. This is because the people have lost the right to stand in the Courts of Heaven. They are not being allowed to present cases because of the *first father's sin* and *mediators' transgressions*. *First father's sin* is speaking of the issues in the bloodline. The devil is using this as a legal right to forbid them from coming into the Courts and presenting a case for their nation. The *mediators' transgressions* means that those who were granted the right to present cases lost that right because of their own transgression, rebellion, and sin. The devil was therefore claiming a legal right to land curses. Curses are always the result of legal ground the devil claims to have. God needs a people to stand in His Courts and revoke and remove that legal claim on behalf of nation. *Reproaches* on a nation means that the accusations the enemy is bringing before the Courts of Heaven against a nation are allowed to stand. In other words, what he is saying he has a right to do against that nation, there is no legal right to stop it. This is because God *needs* a people to partner with Him in the Courts of Heaven. This is on a personal level all the way up to a national level. However, the Lord has made a way for us to be qualified to stand and deal with the first father's sins and transgressions that would deny us the right to present a case. He declared that He would forgive us and cleanse us for *His own sake*. In others words, God doesn't just forgive us because He loves us, though this is true. He forgives us because He needs us. He needs our partnership with Him to see His passion fulfilled and will done in the earth. He needs us to see the restoration of all things that the prophets have spoken. He needs a people who can take the prophetic word of God and claim it before His Courts. When we do this, we are presenting a case that will allow the Lord to fulfill His Word.

> God needs a people to stand in His Courts and revoke and remove that legal claim on behalf of nation.

We see a demonstration of this in Zechariah 3:1-10 where Joshua the high priest has on filthy garments. The result of his garments being unclean is that he has lost the right to represent a nation before the Lord. This was the job of the high priest. He was to stand on behalf of Israel to secure mercy, forgiveness, future, and destiny for them. However, because of the uncleanness, there is no one to do this. The result was a time of restoration was at a complete standstill. God had to remedy this situation. He brought cleanness, forgiveness, and restoration to Joshua. The right to present cases in the Courts of Heaven was restored.

Then he showed me Joshua the high priest standing before the Angel of the Lord, and Satan standing at his right hand to oppose him. And the Lord said to Satan, "The Lord rebuke you, Satan! The Lord who has chosen Jerusalem rebuke you! Is this not a brand plucked from the fire?"

Now Joshua was clothed with filthy garments, and was standing before the Angel.

Then He answered and spoke to those who stood before Him, saying, "Take away the filthy garments from him." And to him He said, "See, I have removed your iniquity from you, and I will clothe you with rich robes."

And I said, "Let them put a clean turban on his head."

So they put a clean turban on his head, and they put the clothes on him. And the Angel of the Lord stood by.

Then the Angel of the Lord admonished Joshua, saying, "Thus says the Lord of hosts:

'If you will walk in My ways,
And if you will keep My command,
Then you shall also judge My house,
And likewise have charge of My courts;

I will give you places to walk
Among these who stand here.

'Hear, O Joshua, the high priest,
You and your companions who sit before you,
For they are a wondrous sign;
For behold, I am bringing forth My Servant the BRANCH.
For behold, the stone
That I have laid before Joshua:
Upon the stone are seven eyes.
Behold, I will engrave its inscription,'
Says the Lord of hosts,
'And I will remove the iniquity of that land in one day.
In that day,' says the Lord of hosts,
'Everyone will invite his neighbor
Under his vine and under his fig tree.'"

The result was all that God intended for Israel was allowed and secured. This could not have been done without Joshua the high priest being reinstated into his place of function.

God needs us. We are critical to His purposes. He will come and cause any and all disqualification to be revoked. He will grant us the right to stand and represent our own lives, families, and assignments we have from Him in His Courts. The result will be curses revoked and reproaches removed. That which has harassed and sought to stop the intent of God will itself be judged.

The encouragement of the Lord to us is to *take our place*. Do not allow any sense of unworthiness or shame to keep you out of the Courts of Heaven. This is exactly what the devil desires.

Come before the Lord and allow the blood of Jesus to cleanse and wash you thoroughly. Forgive yourself even as the Lord has forgiven you. Let the past go and embrace the future that God has created you for. We are necessary to the purposes of God. As we partner with Him as He partners with us, we will see decisions rendered, verdicts set in place, and God's will done.

Do not allow any sense of unworthiness or shame to keep you out of the Courts of Heaven.

Lord, as I come before Your Courts, thank You for the immense privilege and honor of partnering with You. I am aware that You have chosen to allow us this high position and place. I ask that every word against me would now be revoked and annulled by the voice of Your blood. Let me take my place in agreement with You and partner to see Your will done. In Jesus' Name, amen.

Chapter 20

PRACTICAL APPLICATION

PROBABLY the most asked question I get is *how* can I function in the Courts of Heaven practically? My first response to this is, *by faith*. I've come to realize that this simple statement is very intimidating to a lot of people. They feel completely inadequate to do this. They see themselves as too natural or carnal to step into a spiritual dimension and operate there. This is unnecessary. What people don't realize is that they are more spiritual than they give themselves credit for. There is locked up inside of them a spiritual part of them that is willing and ready to function. With this in mind, I want to encourage people to take the prayers in this chapter and pray them with an open mind and heart. As you pray, allow the Holy Spirit to move in you and through you. I think you will be amazed at the revelation and understanding you begin to gain.

ENTERING THE COURTS

Lord, as I come before You, by faith I step into the heavenly dimension called the Courts of Heaven. I enter through the blood of the Lord Jesus Christ that was shed for me. According to Hebrews 10:19, I enter the holiest place through and by this blood. I thank You that because of the blood of the Lamb, I am worthy to stand in this place and present my cases before You.

SUBMITTING MYSELF

As I stand before Your Courts, Lord, I yield and submit myself to who You are. According to James 4:7, I am to submit myself to You as God. The result will be the enemy will flee when I resist. Therefore, I come and humbly yield my being and all that I am to You. I request that according to Romans 12:1-2 I would be an acceptable sacrifice to You, holy and submitted. I ask that I might manifest the good, acceptable, and perfect will of God in and through my life. Search me, O God, according to Your divine inspection and let me be holy and pleasing unto You. Let anything in me that is against You be removed and extracted from my life.

PRESENTING MY CASE

Lord, I now bring my request and petition before this Court. According to Daniel 7:10, I make my request from the books and/or scrolls that are in heaven. From these, I present my prophetic destiny and purpose that was written about me before time began. I also ask that anything resisting my destiny and purpose ordained by You would be judged as illegal and unrighteous. I remind the Courts that the fulfillment of the purpose of God is dependent on my gaining the destiny intended for me. Therefore, I ask that all that is written in my book would now come to pass.

In this phase, you should be mindful of any prophetic understanding you have concerning why you are in the earth.

ANSWERING THE ADVERSARY

Every case against me from my own life and/or bloodline, I now ask that the blood of Jesus would speak for me according to Hebrews 12:24. Let every sin, transgression, deceit, and iniquity be cleansed away from me. I ask that anything the devil is using to legally deny me all that is ordained for me would now be judged as illegal and unrighteous. I repent for any and all claims against me. I ask that Jesus would speak for me according to First John 2:1-2 as my intercessor and propitiation. Let it be recorded that my faith and confidence is in Jesus and His blood. Therefore, I request that every mouth speaking against me would be stopped in Jesus' Name. Lord, I also repent for any and all covenants made with demon powers through sacrifices, offerings, vows, announcements, and agreements with witchcraft. I ask that every altar in the spirit world be torn down, the voice of offerings silenced, and the portals and gates of hell shut. Let them now lose their right to function against me. I also give back anything these powers would claim I have gained through them. I want nothing from them. I only want that which comes from Jesus and what is written in my book in heaven.

As you pray this, be sensitive to any idea, impression, or revelation that you might receive. Repent as specifically as you can. However, don't be fearful about what you don't know. Do everything in absolute faith.

MAKE YOUR REQUEST

Lord, I now stand before You justified through the blood and atoning work of Jesus for me. I request that everything written in my book will now be brought into reality.

Make your request. Be as specific as possible.

RECEIVE

Lord, as I continue to stand before Your Courts, I receive that which is now being released by verdicts, decisions, and the rulings of the Courts of Heaven. I thank You for Your kindness and power to deliver. I thank You that every power of the devil is revoked. His legal right to harass, resist, and hinder are now annulled and dismissed. Thank You that I am coming into the destiny of God written in my book and the book of my family. That which has been delayed is now freed to become mine. I receive it fully now, in Jesus' Name.

LEAVE THE COURTS

Thank You so much, Lord, for allowing me to stand in this holy place. Thank You for allowing me to tread Your Courts and bring my petition before You. As I leave the Courts for this time, I want to again thank You for the blood of Jesus that allows me this privilege. May it be recorded in these Courts that this is my heart and passion toward You. Thank You for allowing me to be Your child and the servant of the Most High God.

In all the practical functions in the Courts of Heaven, always be sensitive and aware of what is being felt, heard, and seen. This can and should be an adventure that is being learned from. These prayers are only guidelines to help you begin. The more you function in the Courts, the less you will need to depend on them. The Holy Spirit Himself will be your teacher and legal aid to help you in the process.

Chapter 21

REPRESENTING NATIONS BEFORE THE LORD

LMOST from the very beginning of teaching on the Courts of Heaven, I was aware of the potential effect upon nations and cultures. I didn't exactly know how this worked, but I was mindful that there was a secret here to see nations unlocked for the gospel. I had an intuitive sense that nations could be freed from demonic intent and brought into their kingdom destiny as *sheep nations* (see Matthew 25:32). As time progressed and the revelation matured, I began to see more clearly what I had intuitively known. I became aware that each of us individually can present cases in the Courts for ourselves and for our families. However, if we were to see cultures shift and change, this required a *house of prayer*. I discovered that a *house of prayer* is essential to presenting cases on behalf of a culture. This means that cities, states, provinces, regions, nations, and continents cannot be freed from demonic rule without a house of prayer representing them before the Lord.

Isaiah 56:7 is a critical piece of evidence to back this up. In this scripture, we see God making powerful promises to the group who would be known as a house of prayer.

Even them I will bring to My holy mountain,
And make them joyful in My house of prayer.
Their burnt offerings and their sacrifices
Will be accepted on My altar;
For My house shall be called a house of prayer for all
nations.

> **The Lord promises to bring those**
> **who are joined to the house of prayer**
> **to the holy mountain.**

The Lord promises to bring those who are joined to the house of prayer to the holy mountain. As we have discussed previously, this is a governmental place in the spirit world. This means that our activity in this place produces shifts in cultures and not just individual or family lives. However, we are told that it is a *house of prayer* that has the right to stand in this place and function. This means it is people who are connected and joined in the spirit world as a *house* or *family*. We are no longer functioning as an individual but now as a *corporate man*. Notice also that it is the house of prayer that represents nations before the Lord. The house of prayer is *for* all nations. In other words, every nation must have within it a house of prayer to go stand and represent it in the Courts of Heaven. It alone has the right to petition the Courts for breakthrough on national and cultural levels.

In the case of Sodom and Gomorrah, we know it was destroyed. What we may not realize is that its destruction was *not* because of its sin. Its destruction was because of the absence of a house of prayer. God agreed with Abraham to spare it if there were ten righteous. This would have constituted a house of prayer to represent this culture. God said they would have had the power to deliver the city from judgment and its fate. Any nation or culture that is represented by a legitimate house of prayer can be saved and become a sheep nation fulfilling kingdom purpose and destiny. However, without a house of prayer representing the culture, its destiny can and will be forfeited. Another thing about a house of prayer for a culture is it must be from within the culture. I always felt it strange that Abraham had such power with God that the Lord would agree to his request concerning the criteria for this wicked place's redemption. I wondered why Abraham himself didn't just request this of the Lord. The Lord then showed me it was because Abraham wasn't *from* Sodom and Gomorrah. The principle is this—*only a house of prayer from within a culture can represent that culture before the Lord.* This is why all cultures must have houses of prayer or a people connected by covenant relationships to stand and represent these before the Courts of Heaven. The absence of this group will cause undue destruction to come to these nations. We must pray and labor for houses of prayer to be raised and take their place in nations.

This is why I started Global Prayer and Empowerment Center (www.gpec.world). This is a *global house of prayer* with representation in nations and cultures. We presently have continental directors in North America, Asia, the South Pacific, Europe, and Africa. These are laboring to see houses of prayer raised from nation to nation and city to city. When these houses of prayer are set into place, they can represent their cultures before the Lord and see the Courts of Heaven render decisions of mercy into place. Also, we can get together even on a global level and have jurisdiction in things that are affecting the whole world. This is why we are Global Prayer and Empowerment Center (GPEC).

We are continuing to pursue the mandates of the Lord concerning the Courts of Heaven and representing them through a house of prayer. This requires people to be joined in covenant relationships with each other. The issue in times gone by is not that we haven't had people praying. The issue is we haven't had houses of prayer bound together in covenant connections. Only when this is in place will the devil not have a legal right to resist us. He will not be able to claim we are not a house. If he can make this case against us, then we will not be able to present cases for nations in the Courts. However, if we are a legitimate house with real connections in the spirit realm, we will be able to stand and present cases. The result will be that God is granted the legal right to render decisions and rulings of mercy to and for nations!

If you would like more information on how to become a part of GPEC, you can go to www.gpec.world. God is forming this global house of prayer to represent cultures and nations before His Courts. We have been raised for such a time as this. Come be a part of this house that has jurisdiction in the heavenlies.

Questions and Answers

Are generational curses a New Testament/New Covenant reality? Where can I find evidence of this?

THE fact is that curses are a reality and they place on people limitations and boundaries not designed by God. From a Courts of Heaven perspective, there are two very important scriptures—Galatians 3:13 and Revelation 22:1-3.

> Christ has redeemed us from the curse of the law, having become a curse for us (for it is written, "Cursed is everyone who hangs on a tree") (Galatians 3:13).

> And he showed me a pure river of water of life, clear as crystal, proceeding from the throne of God and of the Lamb. In the middle of its street, and on either side of the river, was the tree of life, which bore twelve fruits, each tree yielding its fruit every month. The leaves of the tree were for the healing of the nations. And there shall be no more curse, but the throne of God and of the Lamb shall be in it, and His servants shall serve Him (Revelation 22:1-3).

Galatians 3:13 says we were redeemed from the curse because Jesus became a curse for us. However, Revelation 22:1-3, which is about the millennial reign of Christ, says that then and only then will there be *no more curse*. So the question is, when did the curse end? Did it end in Galatians 3:13 or Revelation 22:3? There is actually a simple explanation. Galatians 3:13 is the *stated verdict of the cross*. In other words, it is what Jesus' death set into place legally. However, a verdict not executed into place has no real power. Revelation 22:3 is the *full execution* of the verdict of the cross into place! This will not happen until the new heaven and new earth are in place and the full reign of Jesus is known in the earth. Until that time, we must take what Jesus did for us on the cross and exterminate every curse that would still seek to operate against us and our families. This is what we do in the Courts of Heaven. We execute into place the finished works of the cross.

Can anyone operate in the Courts of Heaven?

Anyone and everyone who belongs to Jesus can operate in the Courts of Heaven. Isaiah 54:17 tells us that we as the righteousness of God have authority in the Courts of Heaven.

> "No weapon formed against you shall prosper,
> And every tongue which rises against you in judgment
> You shall condemn.
> This is the heritage of the servants of the Lord,
> And their righteousness is from Me,"
> Says the Lord.

The word *judgment* is the Hebrew word *mishpat.* This word means "a verdict or sentence." So words and tongues against us can grant legal rights to fashion destinies out of agreement with God's will. We are told, however, that standing in the legal places of the spirit or the Courts of Heaven is our heritage as His servants and our right from the Lord. Do not allow the devil or anyone else to talk you out of the place you have been granted!

Do I need to see or feel something to enter the Courts of Heaven?

Entering the Courts of Heaven is an activity of faith. This means it's great when we feel things, see things, encounter things, etc. However, these are not necessary to be effective there. We do this by faith. This means we take God at His word and begin to live like it's a reality in the unseen world. The truth is, the more you function by faith in the Courts, the more your spiritual senses will activate. You will find yourselves having more encounters as time goes by.

What is the relationship between the Courts of Heaven and the battlefield? How do the Courts of Heaven and spiritual warfare work together?

We have covered this is a previous chapter. I believe it is very dangerous to engage powers of darkness without first removing their legal right of operation. This is how Jesus Himself is said to operate in Revelation 19:11.

Now I saw heaven opened, and behold, a white horse. And
He who sat on him was called Faithful and True, and in
righteousness He judges and makes war.

Jesus first judged, then made war. In other words, Jesus dealt with any legal claim the devil had, then destroyed him on the battlefield. If we are to be successful in spiritual warfare, we must make sure satan's legal claims of operation are revoked. When this occurs, we will easily defeat him. However, if he is attacked before his legal rights are annulled, he will backlash against people and bring great destruction. We must make war wisely.

For by wise counsel you will wage your own war,
And in a multitude of counselors there is safety
(Proverbs 24:6).

Are seers absolutely necessary to getting breakthrough in the Courts of Heaven?

I do not believe that God connects any breakthrough I need to another gift. This always bothered me. If my destiny was tied to a gift I did not have access to, then this seemed unfair. I have come to believe that seers can be helpful but are not essential. Some of the greatest breakthroughs I have received came from direct revelation from the Lord through dreams, impressions, and other prophetic encounters. We must shake free from a sense of inferiority and take up our own cause before the Lord. He will unveil whatever is necessary when we genuinely seek Him.

ABOUT
ROBERT HENDERSON

ROBERT Henderson is a global apostolic leader who operates in revelation and impartation. His teaching empowers the body of Christ to see the hidden truths of Scripture clearly and apply them for breakthrough results. Driven by a mandate to disciple nations through writing and speaking, Robert travels extensively around the globe, teaching on the apostolic, the Kingdom of God, the Seven Mountains, and, most notably, the Courts of Heaven. He has been married to Mary for 43 years. They have six children and five grandchildren. Together they are enjoying life in beautiful Waco, Texas.

INCREASE THE EFFECTIVENESS OF YOUR PRAYERS.

Learn how to release your destiny from Heaven's Courts!

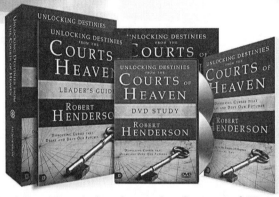

Unlocking Destinies from the Courts of Heaven
Curriculum Box Set Includes:
9 Video Teaching Sessions (2 DVD Disks), Unlocking Destinies *book, Interactive Manual, Leader's Guide*

There are books in Heaven that record your destiny and purpose. Their pages describe the very reason you were placed on the Earth.

And yet, there is a war against your destiny being fulfilled. Your archenemy, the devil, knows that as you occupy your divine assignment, by default, the powers of darkness are demolished. Heaven comes to Earth as God's people fulfill their Kingdom callings!

In the *Unlocking Destinies from the Courts of Heaven* book and curriculum, Robert Henderson takes you step by step through a prophetic prayer strategy. By watching the powerful video sessions and going through the Courts of Heaven process using the interactive manual, you will learn how to dissolve the delays and hindrances to your destiny being fulfilled.